CAUGHT UP IN THE SPIRIT

A Journey from
Complacency to Glory

Christopher Paul Carter

CONTENTS

INTRODUCTION

This book has two major themes. The first is that God is available to us right now, and that means everything He is—all His power, glory, and presence. He isn't waiting for us to get smarter or more spiritual, nor does He need us to exhibit perfect behavior. He wants us to experience the fullness of His presence right now. There is literally no requirement on our part other than to receive the blessing. And when we receive it, a flow of Holy Spirit renewal will change all the peripheral issues that we thought were holding us back.

Through the Holy Spirit, we can experience the same intimacy with the Lord that Adam experienced in the Garden of Eden. We can have the same heavenly encounters that Moses had on Mount Sinai. We can behold the glory of the Lord, up close and personal, just as the disciples did when they were led up the mountain of transfiguration. We have been given limitless access into God's presence.

The second theme of this book is how all the above will be fulfilled in the last generation of Christians. Those "end-times" believers will see the extremes of everything, both good and bad. They will live during a time the Bible calls the "great tribulation," but they will be so close to God's glory, that it will be a joyful experience.

In order to get an understanding of how life on earth will be for the last Christians, we will look at two different people from the Bible, Enoch and Stephen the martyr. They can provide a great prophetic picture of ordinary people experiencing a dramatic connection to Heaven. And, in Stephen's case, doing it under severe persecution.

As we see these two themes take shape, perhaps a bridge can be built between what is available to us now, through the Spirit, and what will be a finalized reality in the last days. And that is ultimately the goal of this book—to show where we are going and to get the journey underway.

Perhaps most important of all, anytime we are dealing with prophetic material like this, we have a responsibility to do some testing. Here is the appropriate word of advice from the Apostle Paul:

> *Do not quench the Spirit; do not despise prophetic utterances. But examine everything carefully; hold fast to that which is good. (1 Thessalonians 5:19–21)*

So, in looking forward to what life might be like in the future, we have to discern through the Holy Spirit. If we take the time to do that He will make it crystal clear what God is saying to us today.

Also, many of the testimonies in this book are spiritual in nature, which means they may go outside the comfort zone of some readers. If that's you, try to keep an open mind. And, at the end of the day, always believe what the scriptures say before anything else. But remember, you have to believe the whole Bible, not just the easy-to-understand parts.

Finally, if at any point you feel yourself wanting to start a journey into the Spirit and you have no idea how, hang in there for the whole story. I don't think learning to experience God supernaturally is instantly easy for anyone, but anyone can do it. That's because God cares for us so much that He won't let our inadequacies get in the way of His love.

Whether at the end of days or right now, God is going to reveal Himself in all His power and glory. Our job is to let Him be God and allow Him to transform us on His terms. When we do that, we will realize that God is far more good than we have ever imagined, and He is bursting at the seams to reveal that to us.

1

THE ENOCH CONVERSATION

One afternoon I was praying in my office when the Lord asked me a very arresting question, "On your death bed, will you be so overcome by My Spirit and My Presence that, right before you die, you will be delighting yourself in My abundance and My glory?"

The question took me completely by surprise, and before I could really get my mind around it, He said, "What about Enoch in the book of Genesis? He was experiencing My Glory on a daily basis until, one day, he translated from this realm to Heaven without the death of his physical body."

God had my undivided attention, and not just because He was talking about my own death. He was reinforcing a concept I had just started learning about—experiencing His glorious presence.

Years before this specific afternoon, God started teaching me to enter His presence when I prayed, and it was still a new process that I was having trouble receiving. So when the Lord started telling me about His abundance, presence, and glory, I was all ears, even though I had no idea how the story of Enoch would fit into the overall picture.

But those two statements instantly encouraged me to press into Him for more, which then started a whole new conversation about knowing God supernaturally, and focusing on how doing so will become the standard in the Last Days.

In a moment or two I'll go into all of that in detail, but first let me see if I can paint a clearer picture of that meeting with the Lord, combined with a little background information about that afternoon.

A New Way to Pray

When I was praying that day, I felt overwhelmed by God's presence. This had started happening more often, and sometimes it even affected my ability to stand up. I would start to feel woozy under the influence of the Spirit of God and, before I knew it, I would have to lie down on the floor and let the Lord pour more of His goodness into me. This happened often enough so that I started laying a pillow down on the office floor in order to have something of a landing pad. The Enoch conversation happened during one of these experiences.

It felt like all of Heaven was smiling down on me and the Lord, Himself, was embracing me. The awareness of how loved and accepted I was in His sight was enough to send me falling to the ground, and it seemed like the more I just laid there and opened myself up to God's presence, the more powerful the flood of His glory became.

I would always be surprised during these times when a vision or a revelation would hit me without any warning or effort on my part. A vision would come and I would be left thinking, "That was the easiest and most joyful thing I have ever experienced!"

I was used to thinking that it would take hours of prayer and fasting and personal effort to be close enough to Him to get a significant impartation from the Holy Spirit. But along the way, I became convinced of another, far more important, reality. My main job was to *receive* while He did all the giving.

Being in God's presence was like getting close to a raging waterfall. No matter where you stood or what you thought about it, you were going to get wet! I liken it to the many pictures of Niagara Falls, showing the boats that carry tourists up close to the waterfall's power and majesty. Even though the boat may be hundreds of feet away from the waterfall, everyone on board is covered from head to toe in waterproof ponchos and rain gear. It doesn't matter if you are far away; the mighty, rushing water falling down on those rocks sprays enough mist into the air to drench everything nearby.

That's what some of these experiences were like. Standing next to the mighty rushing water of the Holy Spirit, you come away from the experience soaked to the bone with revelations, visitations, prophecies, and other side effects of His glory mist. I remember feeling for the first time how much I was loved and how freely accessible all of God's gifts were to me. And above it all, I came away with this sense that God was more "good" than I had ever imagined.

I knew that I had a standing invitation in Heaven, and there was always a divine welcome to come back into the presence of God and interact with Him from within His glory. For lack of a better word, it was delightful. Those were (and continue to be) really wonderful times of communion with the Lord.

Fighting for the Blessing

As I'm sure you realize by now, that kind of experience during prayer was not always a natural part of my communications with the Lord. In fact, just a few years prior to this particular afternoon, I had no real concept of what it would be like to be overcome by the goodness of His presence, or to simply enjoy His abundant love and attention.

I had a slight concept of what His goodness was all about; I certainly would have agreed that God is good! But when the above began to happen, I entered into a season in which it seemed that the Father's first priority was to get me to sit back and become joyfully delighted and remade by His love. God always knows what buttons to push because my overactive and analytical mind found this season to be unnatural.

In fact, my mind easily could have become a major obstacle to receiving something that seemed "too good to be true." Yet, from the first occasion on which I experienced the sense of God's glory, I was hooked. However, I still battled all sorts of thoughts, most of which I once would have considered well-meaning and religious, that kept me from becoming instantly and completely comfortable in this state.

It seemed unproductive and self-indulgent, or just plain wrong, for me to spend my prayer time getting delighted in His presence. Without jumping ahead of myself, I will just say that I fought an intense battle, both within and without. Thanks be to the Lord; once He touches you with something new, you just can't live without it and, over time, it became a natural part of relating to the Heavenly Father.

However, I am sure that the time it takes to comprehend something new like this varies from person to person. For the more stubborn members of the Kingdom, like me, it might take more than a year to stop doubting the new things because of old understandings. So one afternoon, during a season of spiritual discovery that lasted over a year, I found myself in the very familiar position of being overcome by His presence and enjoying Him as we talked and related to one another.

The other all too familiar aspects were the moments of waffling back and forth, wondering if this was a "real" experience (or just emotional nonsense) and if I was right. What I mean by right is, was God really pleased in the way I was praying and interacting with Him, or had I fallen into some sort of spiritual error?

More and more I found myself pushing through the doubts and joyfully grabbing hold of the far more overabundant and joyful interaction with the Father. It was during one of these common moments of struggle and victory that the Lord met me and asked me that odd question I mentioned before.

Trusting His Presence in Death

Now let's go back to the Lord's original question of me that initiated this whole discussion, "On your death bed, will you be so overcome by My Spirit and My Presence that, right before you die, you will be delighting yourself in My abundance and My glory?"

I immediately knew it was the Lord speaking because it left me baffled and was a completely external thought. I wasn't thinking anything close to the statement that soon began racing through my mind, over and over. "On my death-bed . . . will I trust . . . will I delight myself in the glory of the Lord?"

I found this to be a very strange question, but it provoked the following thought. If I were to be in this kind of intimate and heavenly communion with the Lord in the moments before I pass from this realm into the next, then I would have to believe it is real and that this is what God wants me to experience.

Nobody in their right mind would want to meet their Lord and Creator while believing and practicing something that was totally in error. You would not want to meet the Lord with a shock because you believed something fundamental about His character that would turn out to be completely false. Imagine how horrible that would be.

Yet, in this question, the Lord was asking me, "How much do you trust this new intimacy with My Presence? Do you trust it enough that, right before you meet Me after your death, this is what you will believe?"

I knew that the right answer was, "Yes, I do believe it!" It was hard, however, to say that and really mean it because I still had some moments when I honestly wasn't sure if I had lost myself in a fairytale or if I was experiencing something real. However, before I could even wrap my mind around this first thought, the next question rang in my ears: What about Enoch in the book of Genesis? He was experiencing my glory on a daily basis until one day he translated from this realm to Heaven without the death of his physical body.

Enoch's Life and Death

Now I was really becoming interested in where the Lord was going with all this. It would be a huge understatement to say that Enoch's deathbed experience was "unusual." Enoch was one of the few humans in the Bible to skip out on an actual physical death and disintegration. For nearly one hundred percent of humanity, our bodies die and decompose, but Enoch made the leap to Heaven without what we would consider that necessary step.

So, whereas at first the Lord asked me about my own eventual "deathbed" experience, now He had begun to make a related point about Enoch's experience. Here is what the book of Genesis has to say about Enoch's life:

Enoch lived sixty-five years, and became the father of Methuselah. Then Enoch walked with God three hundred years after he became the father of Methuselah, and he had other sons and daughters. So all the days of Enoch were three hundred and sixty-five years. Enoch walked with God; and he was not, for God took him. (Genesis 5:21–24)

I started to envision how Enoch "walked with God and was no more." I saw how he could be in such a strong, intimate communion with the Lord that he was touching the heavenly realm every day. He would have been walking with the Lord much like Adam did before the fall of mankind. Enoch had become familiar with God's presence, and with meeting Him in His glory. When they walked together, Enoch entered into a place in which Heaven and earth touched, where he could meet with God totally unhindered.

For the three hundred or so years during which Enoch developed this intimacy within the heavenly realm, he would walk in and out of the "bubble" in which these two worlds touched until finally, one day, he stayed in the glorious realm. Genesis says that "God took him." It might sound like what could happen only in a science fiction movie, except that it's what really happened to a real person. And even more important than that (as we will see later) is that learning to receive and experience God's glory—by meeting with Him in a way that peels back the barrier between this world and Heaven—is exactly what the Lord wants for us, too.

Enoch had become so familiar with Heaven, and with God's glory, that when he made the transition from this life to the next, it was such a smooth and natural change that his physical body did not have to be abandoned as he left this world. For all of us today the experience of death, which is just the transition of our person from one realm to the next, is such a drastic change in our environment that our present bodies are not suitable. But for Enoch, the transition to Heaven went so smoothly that his body didn't die. It simply translated along with the rest of his persona as he entered into God's glory.

Heaven is a place for incorruptible things, which is why our physical bodies can't go as they are. For a body to go into Heaven, it has to be glorified. The simple way to think about this is that Enoch was so close to God's glory that he was already eternally transformed; not just in his spirit, but in his body as well. With Enoch, nothing was left behind to rot. Everything had already been glorified. That is what can happen to someone who "walked with God" for three hundred years.

Enoch's transition to Heaven occurred far too early to ever be considered natural. Remember that people in his day were living well into their eight and nine hundreds, yet Enoch tallied only three hundred sixty-five years. His early departure was not because his body lacked longevity, but because he was growing so accustomed to living in the heavenly presence that it became natural to stay there and not here.

Enoch's 'deathbed' experience was the easiest, smoothest, and most glory-filled transition anyone ever made from this world to Heaven (not counting Jesus, of course; His death and resurrection take the word "glorious" to a whole new level). Enoch's experience had everything to do with his familiarity and closeness to the glory of God. By the time God took him, Enoch had spent enough time here on earth. So he simply stepped into God's presence one final time and remained there.

Enoch's Path

At this point in the conversation, I had learned a lot more about Enoch than I knew was possible, except by divine revelation. The Bible itself contains only a few mentions of his life and legacy, but the Lord was rapidly filling in the blanks. I remember taking a deep breath and starting to thumb through the Bible. As I did so, the Lord directed me to a verse in Jeremiah.

> *Thus says the Lord, "Stand by the ways and see and ask for the ancient paths, Where the good way is, and walk in it; And you will find rest for your souls. (Jeremiah 6:16)*

I knew the ancient paths God was talking about involved living in His glory like Enoch had done, but what made this verse significant was the realization that what was happening to me was not an isolated event. God had already established a path for living in the heavenly glory.

Saints like Enoch may have pioneered it, but it is a valid and well-established experience. This road has been a around for a while, and God was just now allowing me to see it. I wondered who else had gone down this path, and where they ended up. I knew the end result, if I walked this path to its completion, could be a very unusual death experience.

The last part of the verse gives a little explanation as

to how you might recognize the "ancient path." It is "where the good way is." The word, "good," in our common usage, has become almost meaningless. It means that something is just all right. But to God, the word "good" is fundamental to His whole character.

This whole conversation happened when I was experiencing that goodness on an entirely new level, maybe even for the first time. And just when I thought I had reached the limit, another wave would hit me and show me that He is being good out of a limitless resource of goodness. The ancient path feels good, it causes you to think good, and it spurs you to fully believe that God is good.

When the Lord brought this scripture to my attention, I knew He was saying that Enoch's way of life—the ancient path that he walked with God—was the very thing He wanted me to experience. He wants it to revitalize my earthly experience so completely that it would even affect the way I die. He wants me to experience life as Enoch did, walking with Him everyday inside His presence, and letting His glory saturate my every pore until it changes me inside and out. He wants me to experience Heaven now.

We Can Walk Like Enoch

I was still trying to digest the possibility of experiencing the glory of Heaven before I die when the Lord sent me to the book of Hebrews.

By faith Enoch was taken up so that he would not see death; and he was not found because God took him up; for he obtained the witness that before his being taken up he was pleasing to God. (Hebrews 11:5–6)

This happened with Enoch by faith. This wasn't a case of God choosing someone because of merits, or just to make a point. Enoch was "taken up" by faith. Enoch experienced what he did because of what he believed. He walked with God in His glory because of what he believed. He experienced Heaven because of what he believed. And he was taken up, never to be found by anyone on earth again, because of what he believed. Enoch was not an unwitting pawn in this experience; rather, he was responsible for the whole thing through his faith.

Enoch allowed his desires and passions to take shape in his life. He didn't suppress his longing for total intimacy with God's glory—instead, he put his faith in what he knew was out there. He let himself believe, which is so hard for us today because we don't think God wants us to experience a supernatural life.

We've been taught to sit back and be happy that we're born again. But the Lord is waiting for someone to believe something radical. He would *love* it if we experienced His glory simply because we believed for it. However, this doesn't mean that we are stuck with our own devices when it comes to developing sufficient faith. In the next chapter, we will see how God has a plan to invigorate us, and it has nothing to do with our effort. He will give us the faith to believe the impossible out of His generosity, not because we've drummed it up or deserve it.

Getting back to Enoch, if his story was that of a godly man who drew God's favor and blessing, then it would seem that his translation to Heaven was a really special gift that God gave to one of his faithful servants. Enoch's participation would be only passive, and He would forever be known as a great saint who received a great blessing.

However, the book of Hebrews tells us that he was translated to Heaven by his faith. His experience was not passive at all; indeed, he was already experiencing Heaven on a daily basis as he walked with the Creator. Enoch knew there was a heavenly realm that could be accessed immediately, so he went after it with gusto. That means it's possible for us, too, if we have the same kind of faith Enoch had.

We Have More Potential Than Enoch

If you don't think it's doable, then you're in good company. It is really hard to fully understand and accept the idea that Enoch experienced what he did because he *believed* it, not because it was an unexpected gift.

Most people will say that Enoch (and Elijah, too) got some special treatment, and that they received this miracle because God wanted to give it to them—not because they pursued it. This is the very reasoning that kept my mind from grabbing hold of this revelation. But once this idea had been given some time to bounce around in my head, God upped the ante on me again.

The Lord added, "If Enoch was taken up by his faith, and he did it without the indwelling of the Holy Spirit, what must you be capable of?"

I was stunned. Enoch was translated to Heaven, skipped out on death, entered into the glory in a totally unique way, did it all by his faith, and wasn't even living under the promised blessing of the greatest covenant ever established on the earth. The New Covenant promises us the gift of restoration and fullness in the Holy Spirit. We are to be totally immersed within a part of the Godhead, Himself. If Enoch did it by faith, without the indwelling Holy Spirit, what can we do?

Sometimes it is easy to forget that the covenant we have entered into trumps the glory and majesty of any other. Here is that very point, laid out in 2 Corinthians:

> *But if the ministry of death, in letters engraved on stones, came with glory, so that the sons of Israel could not look intently at the face of Moses because of the glory of his face, fading as it was, how will the ministry of the Spirit fail to be even more with glory? For if the ministry of condemnation has glory, much more does the ministry of righteousness abound in glory. For indeed what had glory, in this case has no glory because of the glory that surpasses it. For if that which fades away was with glory, much more that which remains is in glory. (2 Corinthians 3:7–11)*

The radiance of Moses when he descended from Mt. Sinai was awesome, but ours is greater. The unbelievable fire that fell from Heaven at Mt. Carmel was intense, but the fire within us is greater. The capacity that Enoch had to enter into Heaven and be glorified is simply amazing, but our capacity for the same experience is greater.

It took Enoch around three hundred years of walking with the Lord to experience this. Is it possible we could do it in less time, given that we are walking around every day with a river of God's life rushing inside of us? It may be closer than we think.

A Generation of Enochs

While still praying in my office, I found myself thinking, "Is this real, God? Are you really saying that I am going to experience your heavenly glory like this, and that it is more accessible for me than it was for Enoch?"

But there was still one more installment in this conversation with the Lord that stretched me even further. God had something to say about what is coming on the earth, and how he intends to change our Christian experience in these last days. To do that, He led me to 1 Thessalonians 4:15–17:

> For this we say to you by the word of the Lord, that we who are alive and remain until the coming of the Lord, will not precede those who have fallen asleep. For the Lord Himself will descend from heaven with a shout, with the voice of the archangel and with the trumpet of God, and the dead in Christ will rise first. Then we who are alive and remain will be caught up together with them in the clouds to meet the Lord in the air,

and so we shall always be with the Lord.

The resurrection of the dead has always been exciting to me, but I had never considered the implications of the statement "we who are alive and remain will be caught up together with them in the clouds to meet the Lord in the air, and so we shall always be with the Lord." For every one of these believers, death will be an unknown experience.

When Jesus returns, the believers who are still alive will be snatched up into the sky with Him, and from that point on, they will live in a glorified state with the Lord. They will all forgo a burial and will not participate in a resurrection of the dead. For them there will be no dead body, no eulogy, and nothing left to rot in the dirt.

Imagine an entire world of Christians caught up into the clouds in the blink of an eye, immediately transformed into something bright and eternal. All of them will make the transition into the glory, just like Enoch did. Therefore, when Jesus returns to the earth, there will be a whole generation of Enochs waiting for Him. Every one of them will know the heavenly glory, and they will all be walking with God just as Enoch did.

However, before they are taken up, those Christians will not be living in an easy time. They will have to endure the most traumatic period of distress the world will ever see. Just a casual look at Bible prophecy gives us an expectation for wars, severe natural disasters, and the rise of an Antichrist intent on persecuting God's chosen.

Some believers will surely die during that period of hardship, and some will remain until Jesus returns, but all of them will radiate God's glory in an unprecedented way. We will see, later on, that an intimacy with Heaven will make any kind of death full of glory.

Faith and Power in the Last Days

The final days will be more traumatic than our worst predictions, but in the midst of that crisis, God will be pouring out His glory in such tangible ways that it will redefine what makes a normal Christian life. We are getting ready to enter a time of the greatest miracles and divine intervention the world has ever seen.

However, Jesus asked a question in the gospel of Luke that can be troubling. He asked, "When the Son of Man comes, will He find faith on the earth (Luke 18:8)?" That's a little disturbing coming from the Son of God; does he really doubt that there will be any faithful people left when he arrives?

I am thankful that the question is answered prophetically in 1 Thessalonians 4:15–17. Yes, there will be faith on the earth when He comes. There will be an Enoch faith on the earth, and everyone who survives the winepress experience of the last days will be refined into a group of people who walk with God and are then no more.

The last generation of Christians will live by a supernatural faith that keeps them one step away from entering the heavenly realm, just as Enoch did. When they see Christ in the air, they will not be beamed up into the clouds in surprise, wondering what just happened. Like Enoch, they will have been going in and out of the heavenly realm on a daily basis, making the transition into God's glory a matter of faith and not an accident.

They will be a whole generation of Enochs, and since they will "die" like Enoch, I think it's safe to assume they will *live* like him, too. That is what's coming to those who trust in Jesus. The door has been opened to us to take an ancient path on which we can experience everything Enoch did—and even more. We can learn to live in the heavenly realm, even while we walk around this dirty, corrupted world.

That's what Genesis 5 means when it says that "Enoch walked with God." It isn't a figure of speech, like a way of saying that he pursued God and tried to live a godly life. Enoch actually walked with God, hand-in-hand, in the heavenly places. He lived a life in the spiritual realm that was every bit as real as the natural one.

Starting the Journey

If that seems like an unreachable goal, perhaps you have felt for years that the status quo is all you will ever experience. Many believers have had trouble breaking out of their habitual cycles of ups and downs, and it may feel like you will never live the life of faith you dream of. However, that doesn't mean it won't happen; it just means we need to give God a chance to show us His way of accomplishing it. We need to trust Jesus more, and, once we really begin to see how powerful God actually is, we can learn to lean on His strength and let Him take us on this journey.

God wants to see us connected to Heaven because He loves us and wants us to know Him intimately. So we can believe He has a plan to take us from where we are today to the last generation of Enochs. Step one is to realize where we are right now, and we don't need to kid ourselves. We live in an environment that keeps spiritual things to a minimum and encourages apathy. Modern Christianity doesn't look a lot like biblical Christianity.

That means we have to deal with the complacency we all feel on a daily basis. It's the reason many of us have never been able to sustain a passion for Jesus. If we can deal with that first obstacle, then the door will start to creak open into a far more abundant and supernatural Christian experience.

If we are willing to face our condition, and if we want to start down Enoch's path, then we will see that Jesus has done all the work already. All we need to do is believe Him, which is all Enoch, himself, did.

2

OVERCOMING COMPLACENCY

On my very first mission trip to Europe I had a life-changing adventure with Jesus. I had planned for months to go, had raised sufficient funds, and had convinced a good friend of mine to take the journey with me. I had no idea why the Lord was sending me. All I had was a direction from the Lord to go to England, and He had not yet told me why.

The urge to go came during prayer, and confirmations came through a dream and some prophetic words. I had one very specific word from a member of my home congregation. A young lady told me during a time of commissioning for the trip that she saw the word D-E-R-B-Y.

Since we had asked the Lord in prayer for anything specific that would help, we tucked that bit of knowledge away and waited to see what God would do. Upon arriving in London, it was quickly evident that we had to be determined to make any headway. With only one or two exceptions, the response on the streets was discouraging.

When we finally got a look at a map of England, we saw, right in the middle of the country, the word *Derby*. It was a small town about two hours away by train. We knew we had to give it a shot, so we bought two one-way tickets at the train station.

Prior to leaving, both my associate and I were getting some direction from the Lord. God was telling us to take nothing for the journey, much like He did when he sent out missionaries in the gospels. We were certain that all the Lord wanted us to take was the clothes on our backs and our passports. Somehow, we managed to convince the Lord that it was okay for us to share a stick of deodorant and slip our toothbrushes in our coat pockets.

The day we left I can remember walking to the train station with no money and no luggage, on my way to a city I didn't know existed the day before—all while in another country for the first time. Waiting on the platform for the train to arrive, I was thinking one thing: either God is who He says He is, or He is not. When the train arrived and the doors opened, I stepped on while saying in my heart, "He Is!"

Faith Is Risky

To my knowledge, that was the first time I had ever risked anything for Jesus. I had just become engaged to my wife-to-be eleven days before I left for England, I had no money to get back home on, and I felt a keen sense of responsibility to get my friend home safely as well. However, in that moment, I knew that taking the risk was the right thing to do.

I believe that God will show us demonstrations of power if we are willing to live on the edge for Him, but most of the time we live our lives so "safe" that there is no need for any supernatural involvement. This was the first time I ever thought, "If God doesn't do a miracle here, I'm in some real trouble."

The Bible is full of people who risked their necks for Jesus. They did bizarre things all the time, and it would appear that their radical sense of obedience was always rewarded. One story that I think is often overlooked is the account of the men who went with the Apostle Peter to preach to the gentile, Cornelius.

> *While Peter was reflecting on the vision, the Spirit said to him, "Behold, three men are looking for you. But get up, go downstairs and accompany them without misgivings, for I have sent them Myself." Peter went down to the men and said, "Behold, I am the one you are looking for; what is the reason for which you have come?" They said, "Cornelius, a centurion, a righteous and God-fearing man well spoken of by the entire nation of the Jews, was divinely directed by a holy angel to send for you to come to his house and hear a message from you." So he invited them in and gave them lodging. And on the next day, he got up and went away with them, and some of the brethren from Joppa accompanied him. On the following day he entered Caesarea. Now Cornelius was waiting for them and had called together his relatives and close friends. (Acts 10:19–24)*

I know there are lots of obvious examples of radical faith in the book of Acts, but wouldn't you like to have known the "brethren from Joppa" who went with Peter? Did these unnamed guys have jobs? Did they have families? Did they volunteer? These men took quite a trip! But as a result, the gospel was opened to the Gentiles and the Holy Spirit fell upon them on the spot, shocking Peter and his companions.

It was a definitive success as far as missionary trips go. However, all it would have taken to miss out on that blessing would have been a very sensible comment from the brethren about how they couldn't miss any more work, or what their wives would think if they went gallivanting off with Peter again. All very sensible and reasonable responses to be sure, but all very safe as well.

I know Peter did the preaching and it doesn't say much about these men, but they are perfect, real-life examples of how a risky decision can lead to a life-changing experience. Remember, if you're not willing to risk anything you will never experience the power of God.

Thankfully, my first introduction into risky behavior for Jesus was a success as well. When the train arrived in Derby, it was already getting dark and we had no direction but to walk to the middle of the town and see what would happen. There was no voice from the sky telling us to go left or go right. But there was the unseen hand of the Holy Spirit, guiding us to a church in the town's center.

His hand was also unfelt. It would have been nice if I had been aware of the Holy Spirit's intention, but I really had no idea what was going to happen. For the most part, I felt like we were walking aimlessly—but that just goes to show us how in control God is. Even when we can't feel it, the Spirit is still very active.

While we were standing outside the church building (which was locked and empty), a car came screeching to a halt and a young man got out, wondering what we were doing. The man was one of the church ministers and he just happened to be driving by at the exact moment we stopped to look into the church.

He asked us some basic questions to make sure we were truly Christians, and then he wondered why we were in Derby. To him, Derby was an insignificant city that no one would come to voluntarily, so he was surprised when we told him about the prophetic word we received before we left. Then he looked at us and saw that we didn't have anything but the clothes on our backs.

This prompted the next question, "Where are your bags?" We told him the whole story of how the Lord had instructed us to go with nothing, and now we were here to proclaim His Kingdom.

From that moment on, we were taken to many meetings and Bible studies and we kept giving the same message— God does not think it a waste of His resources to send two men thousands of miles to tell you that His kingdom is near to you. In the years that followed we made many more trips back to Derby, and every time we would be asked to recount the story of our initial visit. It encouraged their faith to know that God was familiar with their "insignificant city" and that He wanted to reveal His love for them.

Coming Home to Complacency

For me and my friend, it was a breakthrough into a new level of trust with the Lord. We never slept on the street and we were always fed and taken care of. Our trip back to London was paid for and we made it home safely a few days later. Even if we had experienced some hardship, it would not have changed our new understanding of how God will supernaturally intervene if we are willing to live on the edge for Him.

Soon after the trip to Derby, we were on a plane back home with our newfound, radical faith and an expectation for more adventures with God. However, upon arriving home, a whole different struggle commenced. Almost immediately, the excitement of our trip was diminished by our comfortable American experience.

If you have ever seen a movie or documentary that depicts the space shuttle reentering the atmosphere, you get a good idea of what it is like coming from a powerful ministry experience back to a complacent society. When the shuttle comes back to earth, the friction between the spacecraft and the increasingly dense air heats everything up, red-hot. And if the shuttle comes in at the wrong trajectory, or if the underbelly is damaged in any way, it could literally burn up as it reenters the atmosphere. The heat is that intense.

It felt very similar coming home to America after living on the edge for Jesus. While we were out in the harvest fields, we were up in the heavens and enjoying a wild ride with the Holy Spirit. Then we came back down. The transition from the heavens back to our normal church experience was intense, and it felt like we were burning up in reentry. This kind of post-trip letdown is a common occurrence. It doesn't have to happen, but the opposition in an apathetic society is so severe that many can't avoid it.

I could feel the draw of comfort and ease as the weeks went on. The television was calling me, along with all sorts of other unnecessary distractions, and I found my radical faith dissipating. To be sure, I had experienced a major breakthrough. I knew how awesome living on the edge for Jesus really was. But that didn't stop me from going back to my old "status quo" faith.

For years after that first trip to England, and as I began ministering in different places in Europe, I kept seeing the same, maddening pattern. Go to Europe; live on the edge of faith; see God do miracles; fall in love with Jesus, more and more; come home; immediately get sucked in to comfort and apathy; finally, get exasperated at my inability to sustain a radical passion for the Lord.

Finding the root cause and a cure for the apathy became an ongoing obsession, and I began to look at different parts of the world for answers. For instance, in countries where Christians are persecuted, you don't hear about problems with apathy. If you live in a place where just *believing* in Jesus can get you killed, you tend to be all-in or all-out. There isn't a middle ground.

Apathy and Complacency

Apathy - Lack of feeling, emotion, interest, or concern.
Complacency - Self-satisfaction, especially when accompanied by unawareness of actual dangers or deficiencies

- From the *Merriam Webster Dictionary*

Reading testimonies of persecuted Christians left me frustrated. They seemed able to live a radical life all the time, while my own faith looked like the stock market timeline. Lots of ups and downs—very little stability. I was left thinking, "What's my problem? What is it in my world that keeps me in an 'average' version of Christianity?"

Here is how the Lord explained it to me. He showed me those areas where violent governments and religions are ready to kick down the doors of the churches and drag all the believers out to kill them or imprison them. In those cases, the persecution is easy to see. It is a physical man or woman doing the oppressing.

Then, God showed me America. There was still an oppressive force bent on breaking into church meetings and dragging everyone away, but it was totally unseen. The attackers were the spiritual forces of apathy and complacency; and they are just as violent and hell-bent as the physical forces our brothers and sisters face in other parts of the world, even though they're nowhere near as obvious.

Complacency is my persecution. It is a spiritual attack that originated in Hell, just like any other form of oppression. Therefore, when I came home from a mission trip back to a wealthy and privileged society, I also came home to a particular set of dark spiritual forces intent on keeping me non-radical. We will talk more about these dark powers later, but here is the scripture verse that describes our struggles with them so well.

Put on the full armor of God, so that you will be able to stand firm against the schemes of the devil. For our struggle is not

against flesh and blood, but against the rulers, against the
powers, against the world forces of this darkness, against the
spiritual forces of wickedness in the heavenly places. (Ephesians
6:11–13 NASU)

There is something in the air above us that wants us
to stay lukewarm and impassionate. It wants us to stay con-
tent with the average and never risk anything for Jesus, and it
doesn't want us to know what it is.

In other words, those dark powers want us to believe
that we are apathetic people because of our circumstances
and our society. They want us to blame our wealth and peaceful existence, and they want us to get frustrated because we
can't break free into a supernatural faith. The last thing they
want is for us to realize we are being persecuted, and that *they*
are the source of the oppression.

We have never been taught that spiritual laziness can
be a product of unseen dark forces, and that has led to some
bad habits and beliefs. If you believe that all the disinter-
est you have in the gospel originates inside of you, then you
will feel very defeated with every year of status quo faith.
However, if you uncover the plans of the "spiritual forces of
wickedness," then you will start to feel empowered, even in
this comfort-driven society.

There is hope for every believer who struggles with
complacency, and it starts with recognizing the source of the
problem. It is a calculated strategy from hell to create a society so concerned with convenience and safety, that the people
are afraid to trust Jesus. We have to see it as our persecution
to have any hope of overcoming it. Then, once the plans of

the devil are exposed, we can receive God's plan to get us out.

For years we have believed the lies and accepted the unseen persecution, which has reinforced apathetic habits and behaviors. In order to get out of the rut, we have to let God show us the way, and the best way to see His plan is to look at the book of Revelation.

The Laodicean Church

Of all the letters to the churches in the book of Revelation, my favorite is the letter to the Laodiceans. They are the seventh and final church to receive a letter from Jesus in John's prophetic account and, in my opinion, the Lord saved the best for last.

I know they get a bad rap, and are often held up as the example of what not to be; but I can't help thinking that if I could be in only one of these churches, it would be the one in Laodicea. They are a great example of where we are as American Christians—and Jesus' words to them should give us hope, even when most readers regard the text from the negative perspective of criticism. For it is precisely their similarity to the church in America that brings so much negative commentary, as we tend to be a little harsh and judgmental with other people when we see things that remind us of ourselves. For example, we are frequently doing this (unconsciously) when we complain about someone's faults— even though we do the same things.

The responses to this letter tend to fit that same pattern. I have heard many sermons about the Laodicean church, and none have been very flattering. Most feature a call to repentance from apathy, coupled with a warning about not being spit out of the Lord's mouth. However, while it's true that the complacent attitude of the church is the first thing mentioned in the letter, it is certainly not the end of the story. This is Jesus' letter to the church in Laodicea:

> *"To the angel of the church in Laodicea write: The Amen, the faithful and true Witness, the Beginning of the creation of God, says this:*

> *'I know your deeds, that you are neither cold nor hot; I wish that you were cold or hot. So because you are lukewarm, and neither hot nor cold, I will spit you out of My mouth. Because you say, "I am rich, and have become wealthy, and have need of nothing," and you do not know that you are wretched and miserable and poor and blind and naked, I advise you to buy from Me gold refined by fire so that you may become rich, and white garments so that you may clothe yourself, and that the shame of your nakedness will not be revealed; and eye salve to anoint your eyes so that you may see. Those whom I love, I reprove and discipline; therefore be zealous and repent. Behold, I stand at the door and knock; if anyone hears My voice and opens the door, I will come in to him and will dine with him, and he with Me. He who overcomes, I will grant to him to sit down with Me on My throne, as I also overcame and sat down with My Father on His throne. He who has an ear, let him hear what the Spirit says to the churches.'" (Revelations 3:14–22)*

This sounds a lot like the apathetic Christianity we find so common in America. Even the subtitle for this section of scripture in some translations reads, "The Lukewarm Church." It would be depressing if that was the legacy your congregation passed on to the next two thousand years of believers.

On the other hand, in my opinion, it is totally mislabeled. It should read something like, "The Church of Visitation." For the most part, however, we have learned about this church because of the rebuke they receive:

> *"I will vomit you out of My mouth. Because you say, 'I am rich, have become wealthy, and have need of nothing' — and do not know that you are wretched, miserable, poor, blind, and naked." (Revelations 3:16 NKJV)*

Just like in America, the Laodiceans were wealthy and believed they had it made. They knew the Lord, but they weren't on fire for Him. I wonder if the Laodicean pastors were constantly frustrated because their congregations wouldn't get motivated to pray and read the Bible consistently, and I'll bet they all struggled to stay passionate for Jesus amid their success and ease of life.

However, I think we have been studying this letter with a preconceived notion that God is spitting them out because of sheer repulsion and is absolutely disgusted to the point of rejecting them. What is really going on is that He has a special blessing for them, which will not only break them out of apathy, but will also usher them into a visitation with Jesus, Himself. The letter to the Laodiceans is not about judgment; it is about giving. The crux of the letter is that God wants to give the Laodiceans something radical, and He wants to do it because He loves them.

If we were God, would we handle apathy the same way? Our typical response to complacency is to want to kick someone's posterior or give them a good pep talk about getting in the game and fighting to the finish. There is something in us that believes the way to cure laziness is to chastise it out, as if all that was needed was more motivation.

If you have ever made a vow to get in shape because of a short-lived conviction, then you know exactly what I mean. For me, all I have to do is watch the movie Rocky and see him training and running through Philadelphia to feel totally inadequate in my physical fitness. The next day I am doing pushups and sit-ups until I feel robust again; but, sadly, this has never lasted more than a few weeks. No matter how much I try to get motivated, the lazy habits always come back, which leaves me feeling even more like a failure. That of course leads to more internal chastisement—Why can't you get it together and get in shape?

The only time I have seen a consistent change in my diet and fitness is when I have let the Lord show me how He sees me. When I get a glimpse of His unconditional love and acceptance, I start to treat myself differently. I begin to love and appreciate my body out of the overflow of love He is pouring into me. However, I have never known any lasting change to occur in response to feeling guilty or emotionally motivated.

It is the same way with complacency and apathy. They are rarely removed by a fire and brimstone speech or, worse, a condemnation. The very nature of complacency makes us immune to that sort of tactic. However, God's plan doesn't involve a motivation speech. It starts with giving and ends with giving. He knows that when we experience the gifts of His glory, unhindered and accessible, it shocks the apathy out of us. Who would have thought that the way to change a lazy and privileged society would be to give them more things?

Unexpected Gifts

As soon as Jesus describes their condition—that they are wretched, miserable, poor, blind, and naked, He then says, "I advise you to buy from Me gold refined by fire, that you may become rich."

When faced with complacency, Jesus will do the one thing no one expects: pile on more blessing. It contradicts the wisdom of the world, which typically suggests that a time of hardship and poverty would be the best way to get the apathy out of this privileged bunch. Jesus is the only person I know who can look at spoiled Christians and say, "The one thing they need is more undeserved favor."

What had they been doing with their last dose of heavenly gifts? Apparently, it made them so comfortable and secure that they forgot how awesome the Kingdom of God is. Yet, the Lord wanted them to experience riches like they had never dreamed of. But instead of more worldly wealth, He took them into the realms of His glory.

It doesn't matter if they squandered His favor in the

past, and it doesn't matter to Him if they don't seem to care about His kingdom. Jesus will not let our indifference curb His longing to make us rich in His Kingdom.

Jesus was probably smiling at them as they read this letter. It must have been shocking to realize that instead of a punishment, God had a blessing. Remember this the next time you feel you have failed at something or have sinned against the Lord. Even if you feel it is so bad it warrants a divine regurgitation, the Lord's response is to offer you even more of His blessing than you had the moment before you stumbled.

That is the awesome truth about His solution for the Laodicean church. God will present you with gifts during the moments He knows you are expecting condemnation. He is determined to lift you up, not bring you down.

Free Riches

When Jesus counsels you to buy gold from Him, he doesn't intend for you to use money; He is giving it to you freely. It is the same principle found in Isaiah 55:1:

> *"Ho! Every one who thirsts, come to the waters;*
> *And you who have no money come, buy and eat.*
> *Come, buy wine and milk. Without money and without cost.*

You can't buy the riches of His glory; you can only receive it. The transaction occurs through the currency of faith. You have to believe that the riches of the Kingdom are in His hands, and you have to believe that God wants you to have them. Learning to believe that God is looking for ways to give you gifts can revolutionize your faith.

The devil has done a great job of lying to us about this subject. He has been telling us we are all one easy sin away from feeling God's wrath. Believers all over the world feel like this everyday, and a good many would-be Christians are held back from putting their faith and trust in Jesus because they think God is looking for an opportunity to drop the hammer of judgment.

In my own life, I was surprised at how much I prayed, ministered, and lived under the assumption that God was more inclined to punish than to give. You don't realize how much the religious devices of the devil have snuck in on you until you experience the freedom of accepting God's gifts. Even more, the Lord doesn't want you to experience them in a trickle; he wants you to get overwhelmed in a flood of His generosity.

Since the Lord is holding His hands out to a complacent, lukewarm church, and His hands are full of blessings that will transform us into something glorious, then I would expect the devil to try to convince us that the "spiritual" thing to do is not to ask for too much.

I have seen whole congregations that have quietly given up on experiencing the glory and power of God because they didn't believe God wanted to give them more than they could possibly imagine. However, when we truly believe it as a foundation of His character, it opens up a door into His presence that allows us to access all that is in the heavenly realms.

I saw the hesitancy to receive God's blessings come out during a meeting with a youth group. This group of high school students had never had a real encounter with the Holy Spirit until just days before, and they were still riding the wave of a first experience with the power of God. They had never seen a prophetic and healing ministry, and were full of questions about how it all worked. I and another minister did our best to field their questions and keep fueling their excitement about what God can do.

The one obstacle that kept coming up was a belief that it was inappropriate to expect the supernatural all the time. When we pressed them about the issue, they admitted that it would be great to experience it constantly, and they did indeed want that, but they were battling an ingrained belief that God doesn't want to give extravagantly.

I got even more specific with them using the example of a prophetic vision. I asked them how many supernatural visions a Christian should expect in a given day. For the most part, they felt one vision was enough—but I could tell they were waiting for someone to say it was okay to want more.

When you think about your own experience, how many supernatural events do you regularly expect? A better question would be, "Why do you expect what you do?" If your hopes are set low, then you need to know that not only is it acceptable to want more Holy Spirit involvement in your life, but God is hoping you will ask Him for it. This is just one example where, even in the face of the miraculous, we have a tendency to think God is not excessive. He is, and He would be delighted if we put Him to the test.

Getting Ready for a Visitation

The Laodicean church went from a miserable and apathetic, yet privileged and wealthy fellowship to one that was known for the glory of the Lord. Think about how Jesus adorned them. He gave them the finest gold, the whitest garments, and an eye salve so that their vision would be perfect. He dressed them like He would His spotless bride, which is what the Church is supposed to be.

The big surprise for the church in America, and all other complacent Christian societies around the world, is that God is about to give us the same rich spiritual impartation. We will be known for the tangible presence of God in our meetings. We will be known as a Christian society whose heart is pure and undefiled, and we will be known as an accurate prophetic voice in our day. But, we have to receive His gifts for that to happen.

At the end of the letter to the Laodiceans, Jesus is standing at the door and knocking. This is not an invitation for salvation, but rather an invitation to let Jesus into the church. Of all the churches mentioned in Revelation, this is the only one that Jesus is preparing for a visitation, which is why I would want to be there. I think we have all been waiting for God to judge the lukewarm church, but the reality is that He has planned a supernatural encounter.

Does that mean there won't be a severe consequence or judgment for complacent Christianity? No, it doesn't mean that. The price for not receiving the free blessings is missing the visitation, which will leave any church or person in horrible shape. Saying no to God's gifts in the coming years will keep you in apathy, and the end result of apathy when it is all played out is apostasy. Later on, we will talk more about apostasy* and what will happen to Christians who don't take time to receive the Lord's gifts of glory.

For now, let's get ready for Jesus' visitation. When we open the door to His smiling face, we will be in for the ride of our lives. Remember, He is not coming in to give us a lecture. He is coming in to give us the riches of His glory and to share a feast. He knows His goodness is the only thing that can change us, and all we need to do is receive it.

***Apostasy** - Renunciation of a religious faith; Abandonment of a previous loyalty.

-From the *Merriam Webster Dictionary*

A Flood of Kindness

It is always good to look at the story of the Prodigal Son in Luke 15 for an example of how God transforms us through His generosity. It also shows us how God is determined to redefine what we think of as a normal expression of love.

The story follows a man who asked for his inheritance and then wasted it with wild living. After a while, the money is all gone and he is left in worse shape than one of the servants in his father's house. He decides to go back to his father and beg for a menial job, just to be able to eat and sleep with dignity. He has no expectation his father is going to be forgiving or appreciate his return; the son is just hoping for a small act of mercy. Their reunion looks like this.

"So he got up and came to his father. But while he was still a long way off, his father saw him and felt compassion for him, and ran and embraced him and kissed him. And the son said to him, 'Father, I have sinned against heaven and in your sight; I am no longer worthy to be called your son.' But the father said to his slaves, 'Quickly bring out the best robe and put it on him, and put a ring on his hand and sandals on his feet; and bring the fattened calf, kill it, and let us eat and celebrate; for this son of mine was dead and has come to life again; he was lost and has been found.' And they began to celebrate. (Luke 15:20–24)

What amazes me about this scene is that the father's first reaction to the son is to give to him. There isn't a lecture that started with, "I told you so," or, "I hope you learned your lesson." The giving starts with kisses and ends with a party in the son's honor.

Surprisingly, the father's welcome isn't based on the quality of the son's repentance. If it were, then he would have let him finish the speech he had prepared—the son only got out about half of what he had intended to say! The father had already planned his son's homecoming, regardless of the attitude of the son when he showed up. After all, the son could have been coming home for no other reason than to ask for more money.

God knows that if he left it up to us, we would never

muster a conviction strong enough to cause us to change, especially in an apathetic environment. His strategy for transformation doesn't hinge on anything we are doing. And if it did, we would be doomed. Like the father in the story, God will give to us before we even know to ask for it.

In this passage, the father starts giving to the son before the son has even had time to see what changed on the farm while he was gone. Also, the son didn't have time to properly say, "I'm really sorry and thanks for the gifts," which shows us how much God's love is not based on our gratitude.

Undeserved Blessings

As we said earlier, God wants us to experience His glory in a flood, not in a trickle. The same was true for the son when he returned. The father's gifts were ridiculously grand. He didn't just give his son a robe, which is a symbol of acceptance and protection; he gave him the best robe he had. He didn't just clothe him; he gave him a ring to put on his finger, which was the sign of his noble authority. He didn't just have a party; he gave him the big party he had been planning for some time. In an instant, he had the son reinstated in his house and back in his honored position, as both ruler and son.

Witnessing an event like that in our day is rare because we live by a different wisdom. If someone had squandered the gifts they had been given and acted completely irresponsibly and unappreciative, we would likely take a more measured approach to that person's restoration. We might forgive, but our trust in the person's ability to be responsible with authority and honor would probably come much later and with more hesitation.

With the Lord, they occur at the same time—*and* it happens before the person has even had a chance to prove a changed nature. It is the same principal we saw previously with the apathetic church. He doesn't need them to be faithful before he gives them gifts only the faithful would deserve.

If a lazy Christian known for a wishy-washy faith came into your fellowship, would he or she be an instant candidate for a position of authority? Probably not. I think we would start by teaching the person to be faithful with the small things, and then we'd wait and see what the person did with the littler tasks.

The honorable positions tend to go to those who have put in the time and have proven themselves to be responsible. That isn't all wrong—the Bible does tell us not to make a new believer an elder in the church. But you don't see Jesus holding people back from ministering and preaching, and I wonder if our reluctance to do the same is part of the reason we don't see more drastic transformation in our congregations. If God is willing to risk his gifts being trampled on by lukewarm saints, I would think He believes the benefits far outweigh the risks.

We need to trust that the Holy Spirit can use people even when we think they are undeserving of great things. God uses unprepared and irresponsible people all the time to prove the Holy Spirit's power, and He does it to break them out of their habitual cycles and move them to new levels of faith.

Jesus has a long history of doing this. The missionaries He sends out in the gospels would have never passed our tests or met our requirements, yet He gave them His full authority and it changed their lives forever. And it changed many other lives as well.

The Cure to Complacency: God's Generosity

Once people have become overwhelmed by His Spirit, it is only a matter of time before they let go of everything that might hinder them. God knows that the best way to release believers from a complacent mindset is to give them more of His glory than they would ever believe they deserve.

Often those gifts of glory come out in strange ways, and one increasingly common sight is the phenomenon of gold dust. For the benefit of anyone unfamiliar with the concept, it is the miraculous appearing of particles of gold on people, in the air, and on anything God wants to give a visible blessing to.

Prior to my acceptance of the Holy Spirit's power, I would have thought that sounded more like alchemy than reality, but God let me witness it with my own eyes. At a revival meeting, two women who were ministering with me came up and very timidly said, "Chris, I think we may have some gold dust on us." I looked over at them, and—sure enough—their faces and hair were covered with flecks of gold. There was no question that they were standing under a window to Heaven.

I studied Physics in college, and I would consider myself an analytical person, so a miracle like this is particularly fascinating to me. It leaves you wondering where the gold dust comes from, since it seems to appear out of thin air. The reality is that Heaven is a lot closer to us than we might think, and the barrier between the natural, seen world and the unseen heavenly world is wafer-thin. So when God wants to release His glory from Heaven, anything can happen. There might be healings, prophecies, and other manifestations that leave us scratching our heads.

All of this is God's way of showing us how much He loves us, and the increasing frequency of this particular demonstration makes me think God is saying to us, "Children, I am running out of ways to show you how good I am, so I have decided to let gold fall from Heaven to convince you that you are loved by a God who knows no limits."

To make His point even clearer, the Holy Spirit spoke to me one day as I sat pondering these signs and wonders. He said to me, "Chris, I am fulfilling my promise to the Laodicean church. I promised to give them gold refined in the fire, and now I am releasing that gold from Heaven." The phenomenon of gold dust is just one way He is pouring out His blessings on complacent Christians.

Do you feel complacent or apathetic? Do you struggle with staying passionate and radical for Jesus? Has your walk with God waxed and waned throughout your whole life? The only way to get out of the rut is to receive His blessings. God's solution is limitless giving, and we will talk about how to receive all that blessing a little later. But for now, stop condemning yourself and stop believing God is condemning you for your apathy. That won't get you out of lukewarm faith.

If you stay condemned in your mind, you will never feel worthy of God's abundant love and supernatural gifts. To find out if that's you, take this quick test. Condemnation will always make you reluctant to approach the Lord, while conviction will make you want to run towards Him with all your might. So, are you hesitant to hold out your hands and say, "God, pour out on me all Your love and generosity"? If you are, it is a sure sign those dark spiritual powers have convinced you that you don't deserve it and that God is mad at you. And if you still think that's true, go back and read about the prodigal son again.

We need an honest look at our situation. We live in an environment in which our spirits are attacked every day, and it is all engineered to keep us unwilling to risk anything for the Lord. Remember, lukewarm faith is as much a product of a dark spiritual influence as it is our wealth and security.

Therefore, if we want to start walking down Enoch's path, we have to give God room to be extravagant. Then we can stop trying to rebuke ourselves out of our apathy, and start letting God give it out of us. Just changing what we believe will start to open the door. God will do the rest.

3

INTO HIS PRESENCE

I was up very late one evening and as I was turning off the lights and getting ready for bed, I took a quick rest on the couch in our living room. The Lord spoke one sentence to me that night, and it was a very clear message. He said, "Friendship begins early." Since it was around 1 o'clock in the morning, I had to ask the Lord exactly what He meant by "early." I am a natural night owl, much to my wife's displeasure, so getting up early doesn't really appeal to me.

When I asked the Lord for some specifics, I knew He was saying to pick a time that would be early enough to consider a sacrifice and make that my time of prayer before the day begins. I chose a time that would be about an hour before I would normally be awake and set out to test this friendship word for a few weeks. Sometimes I would get up early, and sometimes I would hit the snooze button on the alarm, but every time I was able to drag myself out of bed, I had a great time of communion with the Lord.

The strange thing that kept happening to me was that I would wake up about 15 minutes before I had set the alarm to go off. Again, sometimes I would go ahead and get out of bed, sometimes I would go back to sleep and wait for the alarm, and sometimes I would ignore both wake up calls and sleep through the prayer time altogether. But I started to catch on that God was trying to tell me something.

One night, after weeks of being strangely awakened, I decided to put it to the test. I told the Lord that if I woke up again before the scheduled time, I would definitely get out of bed and ask Him what He wanted to say. Sure enough, the very next morning, I was awakened 15 minutes before my alarm rang. I got out of bed and went into my office to pray. As I started to pray, I began thanking God for getting me up and encouraging me to spend more time with Him. I kept thinking, "Lord, I know this must be important, and from now on I am going to try to get up early like You asked me." I thought the whole experience was God's way of saying, "You really need to take this seriously, Chris." I could not have been more wrong.

Surprised by His Passion

While I was praying, the Lord spoke in a clear, calm voice. "Chris, I am not waking you up because I am serious about you learning to get up early for prayer. I am waking you up because I am so excited about meeting with you in the Holy of Holies that I cannot contain Myself. I can't wait for your alarm to go off, and I am stirring you out of bed so we can steal just a little more time together."

I was totally bewildered at what God had just said, and the first word out of my mouth was, "Really?" It seemed so far-fetched that God Himself was that eager to commune with me. Was I to believe He was poking me while I slept because the anticipation of our time together was too much for Him? Do we even have a category, as good Christians, for the God of the Universe being so overcome by His love for us? I certainly did not, and that's why that morning completely changed my understanding of the Lord.

I had no idea how much the Lord desires our interaction. Does He have to have it? No. He is the Lord and He doesn't need anything. He is sufficient all by Himself. But He wants it. He wants us to be near Him so much that it can actually overwhelm even His sense of patience. He could not wait for me to get up with the sound of my alarm. The prospect of my entering into His presence was a delight to Him, and He wouldn't wait for a machine to tell me it was time. He wanted more time with me, and He stirred me up for weeks to get that message across.

I didn't say much in prayer after that. I was so awestruck by this new information that I couldn't even move. It was one of the first moments that I realized God was much, much better than I ever imagined. I didn't have an understanding of God as an intensely emotional being, so I was completely shocked by the Lord's very candid response to my test.

Our religious mindsets do a good job of painting a picture of God that is distant and unreachable. Thinking about God as passionate and excitable seems less spiritual to us, and that should show us just how "religious" we really are. We don't like to think that God is capable of excess because we have suffered so much from our own misguided overindulgence. But He is absolutely excessive in His love for us. He will never be satisfied with us knowing Him from a distance. He is always trying to get us to come in closer to Him than ever before.

Meeting in the Holy of Holies

When the Lord said He was excited about meeting with me in the Holy of Holies, He was being very specific. The Holy of Holies, in the Old Testament, was the one place the head priest would go to meet with God in His glory. It was a place of total transparency with the Creator.

Before the Holy of Holies was built, Moses set the example for meeting with God when he went into the tent of meeting and talked with the Lord face to face. It was such an open and intimate communication that the Bible speaks of Moses meeting with God as a man would meet with his friend. Through Moses, the Lord initiated the building of a tabernacle in which His glory would reside, and where He would communicate with His people. When God directed the design of the tabernacle in Exodus, He specified three different areas, the innermost being the Holy of Holies. Here is a description from the book of Hebrews that summarizes its design and features:

> *For there was a tabernacle prepared, the outer one, in which were the lampstand and the table and the sacred bread; this is called the holy place. Behind the second veil there was a tabernacle which is called the Holy of Holies, having a golden*

altar of incense and the ark of the covenant covered on all sides
with gold, in which was a golden jar holding the manna, and
Aaron's rod which budded, and the tables of the covenant; and
above it were the cherubim of glory overshadowing the mercy
seat (Hebrews 9:2–5)

The structure of the Holy of Holies is a shadow of
God's throne room in Heaven, which the Lord emphasizes
throughout the Bible. Whenever someone received a vision
of the throne of God, such as Isaiah, Ezekiel, and John, there
was always an order to what they saw that matched up perfectly with the structure of the Holy of Holies. They all saw
a group of cherubim or seraphim (different orders of angels)
surrounding the throne and declaring the holiness of God.

Despite what we have all seen in artwork, a cherub
(singular of cherubim) is not a chubby baby. Cherubim are
glorious creatures at the top of the angelic order. To get a
sense of how different they are from those rosy-cheeked little
cupids, take a look at a description from the book of Ezekiel:

Within it there were figures resembling four living beings. And
this was their appearance: they had human form. Each of them
had four faces and four wings. Their legs were straight and their
feet were like a calf's hoof, and they gleamed like burnished
bronze. Under their wings on their four sides were human
hands. As for the faces and wings of the four of them, their
wings touched one another; their faces did not turn when they
moved, each went straight forward. As for the form of their
faces, each had the face of a man; all four had the face of a lion
on the right and the face of a bull on the left, and all four had

the face of an eagle. Such were their faces. Their wings were spread out above; each had two touching another being, and two covering their bodies. (Ezekiel 1:5–11)

On the top of the Ark of the Covenant, which was in the Holy of Holies, were fashioned two cherubim. It was between these two cherubs, on the mercy seat, that the Lord would show up in a cloud of glory. Here are just two of the scriptures that describe that scene.

And there I will meet with you, and I will speak with you from above the mercy seat, from between the two cherubim which are on the ark of the Testimony, about everything which I will give you in commandment to the children of Israel. (Exodus 25:22 NKJV)

Give ear, O Shepherd of Israel,
You who lead Joseph like a flock;
You who dwell between the cherubim, shine forth!
(Psalms 80:1 NKJV)

Whenever the Lord reveals Himself in His glory, a group of cherubim precedes and surrounds Him, just as they do in the representation in the Holy of Holies. They are the Lord's secret service, if you will—the elite angelic order that announces, protects, and amplifies the awesome purity of His presence, if "amplifying" His purity is even possible.

Also, the Lord doesn't need protection, but there could be a need for some buffer to separate the Holiness of God from the rest of creation. I have often wondered if the cherubim might not be there to prevent some cataclysmic reaction between the naked power of God and a fallen world.

If you have ever read anything about matter and antimatter, you know scientists theorize that if these two things came together, it would release an enormous amount of destructive energy. Would it be like that if the cherubim weren't there to put some distance between the throne and the world? Who could know, but there isn't a single example in the Bible of the throne of God manifesting without these special creatures in attendance. Nothing gets past these beings; in terms of physical positioning, they are the closest living entities to the throne of God. Beyond them is the infinite, unquantifiable presence of the Almighty.

We can see them guarding the presence of God all the way back in Genesis, when Adam and Eve fell and were expelled from the garden. The Garden of Eden was a place of unhindered relationship with the Lord, where both man and Creator walked together in intimacy. The nakedness of Adam and Eve was paralleled by the unveiled presence of the Lord. But as soon as sin entered the picture, the intimacy of the garden became off limits and man had his first recorded encounter with a cherub. The Lord placed one (or more) at the entrance to the garden and armed him with a flaming sword to keep man out. This was also Adam and Eve's first experience with a barrier between God's glory and the rest of the world.

> Therefore, the Lord God sent him out from the garden of Eden, to cultivate the ground from which he was taken. So He drove the man out; and at the east of the garden of Eden He

stationed the cherubim and the flaming sword which turned every direction to guard the way to the tree of life (Genesis 3:23–24).

Thus began humanity's separation from God, which went on for millennia until the advent of Jesus Christ. What's interesting, though, is that man's first recorded encounter with a cherub might have left a lasting, somewhat painful impression. They were at the entrance to the garden to keep man from reentering into a perfect relationship with the Lord. This is not to say that the cherubim were somehow mean or obtrusive. They were just doing their job to surround the holiness and purity of the Lord

So, from the very beginning, the cherubim were a buffer between God's perfect, unveiled power and mankind. The presence of the cherubim on top of the Ark reinforced that. Remember, God said He would meet with Moses from between the cherubim. They were still acting as the buffer. But God always has a plan, and there was no way He was going to let mankind continue to live without providing a way to get back to the perfection of the Garden.

Nothing to Separate Us

That brings us to Jesus. His death and resurrection were the events that broke the barrier between man and God, and there are a few things we can look at to see how it brought us back to an unhindered relationship with Him.

First, the gospels tell us of the curtain between the Holy of Holies and the rest of the temple being torn in two when Jesus died.

> *And Jesus cried out again with a loud voice, and yielded up His spirit. 51 And behold, the veil of the temple was torn in two from top to bottom; and the earth shook and the rocks were split. (Matthew 27:50–52)*

Right then, at Jesus' death, the veil that shielded the Holy of Holies from view was split in two. When you think of the veil as the "garment" covering the Lord's naked power, and you know that it would be totally normal for a Hebrew to tear his garments in mourning, it is easy to see why some scholars have seen this as Father God ripping His garment because of the death of His Son.

That is a powerful interpretation of the event. It is also widely believed that the torn veil was God saying, "The way into the Holy of Holies is now open." From the book of Exodus on, the Holy of Holies was guarded by that veil. And at this moment, anyone standing in the temple could see right into the sacred place that was previously off limits.

That was a very big change, and it certainly speaks of a restored relationship with God. But Jesus' work on the cross restored us back even further. His full victory at Calvary took us all the way back to the Garden. Let me explain how.

Not long after Jesus rose from the dead, He sent the Holy Spirit to the believers on the day of Pentecost. On that day, God put an actual part of His glorious persona inside man. The advent of the Holy Spirit into mankind empowered the believers in such awesome ways that the only way to fully appreciate it is to read the whole book of Acts for yourself. But the significance of the blessing of the Spirit went far beyond the healings, signs, and wonders. It brought us back to a relationship with God that has no barriers.

If you have received the Holy Spirit, then you have a deposit of the perfect Spirit of God inside of you. That means the Lord places a part of His awesome, divine self inside each person who is willing to accept His promised gift. That, in and of itself, is a pretty big game-changer. But being full of the Spirit also made it possible to experience a whole new state of being that is never discussed in the Bible until after the advent of the Holy Spirit.

> *I say then: Walk in the Spirit, and you shall not fulfill the lust of the flesh. (Galatians. 5:16 NKJV)*

> *With all prayer and petition pray at all times in the Spirit (Ephesians 6:18)*

> *I, John, your brother and fellow partaker in the tribulation and kingdom and perseverance which are in Jesus . . . I was in the Spirit on the Lord's day (Revelation 1:9–10)*

Doing something "in the Spirit" was only written about after the Holy Spirit fell on the believers in Acts, Chapter 2. There is, in fact, one possible reference to the same concept in Ezekiel 37, and a few mentions in the gospels, but the rest of the 45 or so uses of the phrase "In the Spirit" are post-Pentecost. Since that event, not only is it possible to be full of God's Spirit, but we can also experience life within His Spirit, too. So, two things happened in that very important moment in human history. We received an incredible gift—the Holy Spirit. And that gift made it possible for all of us to walk, pray, and be in the Spirit.

Now, let's go back to the cherubim. Remember, they have been there from the beginning, at the Garden of Eden, to separate the fallen creation from the perfect purity of God. Well, the Holy Spirit provides us a way back to the intimacy of the Garden.

If you are "in the Spirit," then you are relating to God from within a part of His Trinity—the Holy Spirit. So, wherever the Holy Spirit is, you can be too, if you are in Him. That is why the advent of the Holy Spirit is such a drastic change. It made our relationship with God internal instead of external. We don't have to look at God from behind a barrier anymore, whether it is a veil or a protective circle of angles. We can experience Him from within a part of Himself.

Sitting on the Throne

To take this a step further, let's look at the book of Revelation to see the invitation to enter into God's glory and experience Him from the center of His throne. Once again, we can look to a promise for the Laodicean church to understand how God wants to give us a special blessing.

"He who overcomes, I will grant to him to sit down with Me on

My throne, as I also overcame and sat down with My Father on His throne." (Revelation 3:21)

Can you imagine talking with God from the center of His throne? It will be a glorious day when we have "overcome" and are sitting down with Christ in our glorified bodies; yet, even now, we can experience the same thing through the Spirit. If God is sitting on His throne, and we are relating to Him from within a part of His Trinity, then we can be right there with Him in the Spirit!

As we go on, we will talk more about experiencing God in the Spirit. To be sure, it is altogether different than experiencing something in the physical dimension. However, all five senses still work in the unseen, spiritual realm; it just takes some time and practice to learn to use them that way. The fact is that, in the Spirit, you can walk with God in the Garden and talk with Him from the center of His throne—that is all part of the blessing.

We are allowed to experience Him while sitting on the same throne that is constantly surrounded by powerful cherubim. We are so special in His sight that He allows us to see His glory from within the circle of elite angelic guardians that are the last buffer between His absolute absoluteness and the rest of creation.

When the Lord gave the instructions for the Ark of the Covenant and the place of the mercy seat in Exodus, I imagine Moses and the priests after him were shocked to be allowed to approach the cloud of glory at all. No wonder the Lord says that the new covenant has a greater glory. We now experience the Lord from within the cloud of His presence. Now we can be between the cherubim, where the Lord dwells.

It is all about intimacy with Him. God wants us to experience Him in the closest way possible, and He is always drawing us in closer and closer. He wants to sit us on His throne of love, authority, and power, because to Him we are just that special.

> *Therefore let us draw near with confidence to the throne of grace, so that we may receive mercy and find grace to help in time of need. (Hebrews 4:16)*

God Is a Romantic

That morning, when the Lord told me why He was waking me up early, I was struck speechless by His love for me. He wanted to commune with me in the midst of His throne, from within the glory and in between the cherubim. I caught one of my first glimpses into His desire to talk with me like He did with Adam, with no barriers between us. I also saw just how much He desired relationship. It made Him so exuberant that He hardly seemed like the God I had learned about most of my Christian life.

While I was digesting all of this, He reminded me of a scripture in the Song of Solomon:

> *I was asleep but my heart was awake.*
> *A voice! My beloved was knocking:*

'Open to me, my sister, my darling,
My dove, my perfect one!' (Song of Solomon 5:2)

I knew this is what was happening to me as I slept. I was being stirred by my beloved like a bride being called by her bridegroom. I saw a picture of the Lord throwing rocks at my window, trying to coax His beloved to come out and meet with Him. It made me smile to think that the Lord is that young at heart. He can even be playful at times, in His adoration.

If we don't have room in our Christianity for the Lord to be adoring and passionate, we will likely miss the invitation into His glory. There is no way to enter into the intimate presence of the Lord if you believe Him incapable of excessive demonstrations of love. If you don't know just how much He likes you and is moved to joy because of you, it will be impossible to believe the invitation is real.

Seeing the Lord Rejoice

The Scriptures contain some other great examples of the Lord's exuberant love. One of my favorites can be found in the book of Zephaniah, and I often go back to this passage when I need to be encouraged. It is a word of restoration to a down-and-out people. It is also a great picture of how God responds to us all the time. No matter what is happening in our lives, the Lord does not change. These verses comprise one of the best examples of how God feels about you, right now and forever.

> *"The Lord your God is in your midst,*
> *A victorious warrior.*
> *He will exult over you with joy,*
> *He will be quiet in His love,*
> *He will rejoice over you with shouts of joy. (Zephaniah 3:17)*

I always get reenergized when I think about the Lord being near me and rejoicing over me. It is encouraging enough just as it's written here, but the English translation doesn't do this passage the justice it deserves. In the original Hebrew, the words "He will rejoice over you with shouts of joy" literally mean to twirl and spin around under the influence of a violent emotion. It isn't just a shout or a hallelujah. It is a total, full-body moment of exuberance. This rejoicing looks more like someone lost in a frenzy of excitement than the more controlled celebration we often imagine. In this moment, God, Himself, is under the influence of violent emotions, and His physical response is not at all contained.

Have you ever thought of the Lord like this? Can you picture Him lost in a whirlwind of excitement and joy? Can you see Him being so overcome by His emotions that He looses the control we all think would befit someone of His divine stature?

It is in perfect keeping with the words God spoke to me the morning He woke me up before my alarm. He is far more energetic and excited about us than we have ever realized. When He expresses how He feels, we are often left dumbstruck, just as I was, at how much His love seems to get the better of His self-control.

If you have never seen the Lord dancing, twirling, and shouting His adoration above you, then I would invite you to ask for a vision the next time you are praying. Ask the Lord to let you see Him as He rejoices over you. It can be shocking to see the Lord of creation in a moment of unrestrained joy. It is also very contagious. The first time He opened my eyes to see His joyful display, I also got caught up in the praise. I started to mimic the dance I saw Him doing, which involved me spinning around in my office with a gigantic smile on my face.

Experiencing God's Smile

I had a dream one night that showed me again how much God wants to remove all the hindrances to His glory. The dream started with me and a friend driving down the road in our car. It was nighttime, but in an instant it was completely bright outside, as if it were the middle of the day. The change was so drastic and immediate that many of the other cars on the road pulled over to try to figure out what was happening. We were shocked as well as we pulled the car over and got out. I saw people looking at the sky in bewilderment, and I saw some others pointing all in the same direction to the horizon.

I looked at where the people were pointing and saw the skyline of a city. I could see the skyscrapers and buildings as if I were a few miles away. Then, as I watched, a huge eruption burst up from the ground and spewed black smoke everywhere. It almost looked like a volcano exploding in the heart of the city.

While I was watching the explosion, Jesus walked across the earth right in front of me. He stood thousands of feet tall; He was so tall that when I looked up at Him, He appeared to be tapered at the top, just like a tall building appears when you look up at it from its base. He crossed my entire field of view with one stride of His legs.

I have never felt such a strong sense of dread in any dream prior to this, and the sight of Him striding across the earth filled me with so much holy fear that I dropped onto the asphalt beside our car. I could actually feel the asphalt on my nose as I lay face down, afraid to move. The only thought I kept repeating in my head was, "Oh God, I just hope I am saved."

There was no doubting in the dream that this was the Last Day, and if you hadn't made the cut before now you had lost your chance to be in God's Kingdom. I had no thoughts about an eternal reward, a mansion in Heaven, or a crown filled with jewels. I was only concerned with the most basic condition of my soul. The sheer awe of witnessing this event was enough to scare the non-essential issues out of my mind.

Immediately after Jesus walked out of my field of view I saw something getting out of the ground beside me. I was still pressed nose-down on the road, but out of the corner of my eye I watched something rise up from the ground. Then, I saw two dirty feet walking in front of me, going the same direction Jesus was going. I knew they were the people God had raised from the dead and they were going with Jesus to celebrate His Kingdom.

I still hadn't moved a muscle since I saw Jesus. While I was lying there, hoping I had made it into the Lamb's Book of Life and that I would be spared, I felt two hands on my face. Each hand was cupping one of my cheeks and raising my head up off the ground. When I opened my eyes, I was looking into the face of Jesus.

He had the biggest smile and looked at me with the most compassionate and welcoming eyes I had ever seen. Immediately I turned away from Him and broke my face out of His grasp. I felt so unclean and unworthy. It didn't seem right for me to be looking into the face of the Lord. Then, His two hands grabbed my face again and turned me to look at Him. He still had that smile that looked almost playful, and I could feel Him communicating with me even though His mouth never moved.

He was saying to me, "Chris, you don't know how saved you really are. You are clean and pure in My sight, and you have nothing to be afraid of." The dream ended with me looking into His face and taking in that enormous smile. Since then, when I have described that dream to other people, I tell them how His smile is the one thing I remember the most. It was joyful to the point of laughter.

He knew He was confronting my serious and religious mindsets, and that delighted Him. He had the smile of someone who is giving a gift that is totally unexpected and overwhelming. If you have ever done that for someone, you know how your face hurts trying to hold in the excitement. Look in the mirror the next time you do it to see what I am talking about.

That dream was a great insight into the day of Jesus' return, and it followed the prophetic scriptures perfectly. The night turned to day in an instant (Zechariah 14:7). Then the Lord appeared in His majesty and the dead in Christ rose first (1 Thessalonians 4:16). For me, it was also a much-needed revelation about acceptance. I didn't need to be afraid or concerned about my own salvation, and I didn't need to be hesitant to look into the face of God.

He is sending us the message in these days that we can approach Him with all confidence. He is not holding anything back from us, and He wants us to meet with Him in His glory. He wants us to behold His face and speak with Him from the center of His throne. He wants all of our religious tendencies that portray Him as stoic and reserved to be lost in His smile.

The Lord knows that when we start to experience the fullness of His presence, we are going to be filled with more glory than we can contain. Just as Enoch did, we will learn to have one foot in the heavenly glory and one still on the earth. We need to remove every obstacle in our minds and hearts that prevents us from meeting with Him between the cherubim, and it all starts with believing He wants you in His presence more than anything else in the world.

4

RECEIVING HIS GLORY

Everyone likes to feel good. Because, feeling good feels . . . good! When we come into God's kingdom, we can sometimes tend to think that feeling good is now a thing of the past—and there are a lot of religious teachings out there that support this. Maybe it's because we think that taking up the cross and following Jesus means a lifelong pursuit of self-denial that will rob us of any joy or fulfillment.

While the part about self-denial is certainly necessary, a life devoid of fulfillment is not God's plan. The truth is that God made us to feel good. He is the one who gave us the capacity to feel that way in the first place. It is there by design. In the Garden of Eden, all Adam and Eve felt for that timeless period before they sinned were good things. The physical, spiritual, and emotional ability to perceive that something was good, and then to bask in that state of being, was engineered into us by the Creator Himself.

Simply put, God is good and He created us in His image. So, all that man experienced in the perfection of the Garden were the good things of God. Wanting to feel good is not a product of the fall of mankind; on the contrary, feeling anything but goodness is the fruit of the fall.

God delights in His children more than anything else

in this world, and as we talked about earlier, He gets overwhelmed with joy when He has their undivided attention and affection. Accordingly, when we are in His presence we are overwhelmed with joy as we gaze upon His beauty and majesty.

I have never heard anyone who has experienced a close encounter with God say that they have had enough. Everyone wants to go back immediately for more. Well, maybe not immediately. There is normally a short period of slack-jawed unbelief at what has just happened, but no one has experienced a taste of His brilliance and then been satisfied. We always end up wanting more. And that is the key. God made it so that spending time with Him feels better—on every level, not just emotionally—than anything else in all of His creation.

The Lord knew that if something felt better than spending time with Him, we would end up worshiping that very thing. Many of us feel confused after hearing that statement, because it really does seem like there are things in life that make us feel better. The proof of this is in our reluctance to pray, compared to our appetite for television or other replacement things.

Because we were made to feel good, we always look to have our hunger for goodness satisfied, and we will fill that void with whatever we think will do the best job. So, we eat, watch things, and do things that we believe will make us feel the best. But it isn't a case of these things actually feeling better than meeting with God; it's that most of us have never really done so. It's our ignorance of His presence (and what that really feels like) that leads us to experience goodness in all the wrong places.

Many people have a hard time cultivating a life of prayer because prayer doesn't feel good. If it felt as good as it is supposed to, then people would be late to every appointment in their daily routines because they would pray too long. More often than not, though, prayer feels like drudgery. It brings up bad thoughts, feels boring, and doesn't satisfy. All this can change, however, by learning to get in His presence.

Also, there are a whole host of dark spiritual powers that are trying to keep God's kids from experiencing His glory, and we will look at a few of them a little later. Suffice it to say, they are continuously inventing things to mimic the feeling of His presence. One evil invention that drives this point home is the drug, heroin. When people take it, they report feelings of total euphoria and elation. It is considered by some to be the best feeling they ever had, which, of course, keeps them coming back for more. Sound familiar?

Heroin is the devil's perverse and wretched attempt to recreate the way a person feels when they enter into the presence of God. It gives the user a chemically-produced imitation of the glory, and then leaves them imprisoned with addiction and tormented by evil spirits. It is an effective trick because the devil understands something we have ignored: meeting with God is euphoric, and we are longing to experience that kind of connection with Him.

Moses, the Goodness, and the Glory

Moses was a lot like Enoch in that he had a close relationship with the Lord that left him totally transformed. Even though Moses never had a bodily translation, he still experienced the effect of God's glory on human flesh. On one occasion, His face glowed so brightly after viewing just a small portion of God's glory, he had to wear a veil to protect others looking upon *him*. Moses was one of only four biblical examples of a human being glowing because of a glory infusion: Moses, Elijah (on the Mount of Transfiguration), Jesus, and Stephen.

Let's take Jesus out of the discussion for the moment, because he was the actual presence of God in bodily form; and Elijah is a bit of a mystery because he appears in a glorified form with Jesus, but there is no record of his glowing during his earthly life. That leaves just Moses and Stephen as men who glowed prior to death—for sure! They must have had some intimate knowledge of God's glory for it to already start altering the metaphysical makeup of their bodies. We will talk about Stephen later since he is a great prophetic picture of the church in the last days. For now, let's look at Moses' encounter with God to see how God introduces a man to His powerful presence.

> *Then Moses said, "I pray You, show me Your glory!" And He (the Lord) said, "I Myself will make all My goodness pass before you, and will proclaim the name of the Lord before you; and I will be gracious to whom I will be gracious, and will show compassion on whom I will show compassion." But He said, "You cannot see My face, for no man can see Me and live!" Then the Lord said, "Behold, there is a place by Me, and you shall stand there on the rock; and it will come about, while My*

glory is passing by, that I will put you in the cleft of the rock
and cover you with My hand until I have passed by. Then I will
take My hand away and you shall see My back, but My face
shall not be seen." (Exodus 33:18–23)

Moses cried out to see the glory of the Lord, and the Lord immediately said, "I will make all My *goodness* pass before you." God answered Moses' request perfectly. It just so happens that God's *glory* is the same thing as His *goodness*. The change in words was not the Lord playing slight of hand; God gave Moses exactly what he asked for.

It would be really easy to think that—via the word change—God was really saying, "You can't handle My glory so I will just show you My goodness." However, the revelation for Moses was that seeing God's goodness *was* seeing His glory. The word change is so specific that, at the end of the above passage, the Lord goes back to using the word glory to describe what Moses is about to see. With God, these two words are interchangeable.

So, if we want to reconnect with God's presence, which will mean experiencing His glory from the center of His throne, then step one will be to reconnect with His goodness. God will respond to us the same way He did with Moses, and that is a much-needed revelation today. We are far out of touch with how good He is, which is why many, many Christians doubt He will fulfill their every need, heal their sicknesses, and condescend to them with His presence.

But just imagine being in Moses' shoes when all of God's goodness passed before him. Not just a sliver, but all the goodness of the Lord! It is no wonder that Moses had to be hidden in the cleft of the rock and covered by God's hand—that is a lot of goodness to try to take in. One would think it would be an awesome, frightening, and just maybe a euphoric experience all at the same time.

Following the display of glory/goodness comes the proclamation of God's name (Exodus 33:19). This was also a calculated demonstration to get Moses in contact with how good God really is. The name of the Lord comes out as a multifaceted character description. Take a look at what is recorded in Exodus 34:5–9:

> *The Lord descended in the cloud and stood there with him as he called upon the name of the Lord. Then the Lord passed by in front of him and proclaimed, "The Lord, the Lord God, compassionate and gracious, slow to anger, and abounding in lovingkindness and truth; who keeps lovingkindness for thousands, who forgives iniquity, transgression and sin; yet He will by no means leave the guilty unpunished, visiting the iniquity of fathers on the children and on the grandchildren to the third and fourth generations." Moses made haste to bow low toward the earth and worship.*

Now consider the various parts of His name in the order in which He gave them:

The Lord

The Lord God

Compassionate and Gracious

Slow to anger

Abounding in loving kindness and truth

Who keeps loving kindness for thousands

Who forgives iniquity, transgression, and sin

He will by no means leave the guilty unpun-
ished

Visiting the iniquity of fathers on the children
and on the grandchildren to the third and
fourth generations

To me, this name reveals much more than His attri-
butes. It also reveals how God wants His children to get to
know Him. The first two names are obvious, and many of us
address God as Lord when we pray. However, it might change
things up a little if you start your prayer with, "Dear Compassionate And Gracious." Or even, "Dear Slow To Anger." All
of these are legitimate titles that He is known by, so it is fair
game to call on Him by any of these names.

The message to Moses in this proclamation can
also be found in the specific order the names are given. For
instance, if someone on the street asks for my name, I say,
"Chris." If they press me a little more I might say, "Christopher." If they keep asking for more information I will add on
the following:

Christopher Carter

Christopher Paul Carter

Christopher Paul Carter, son of Paul and Debbie Carter...

You can see the pattern. Everyone in my daily life knows me as Chris. That is the name I am known by in most normal interactions. I don't really want to be called by my full name when my wife greets me; I want to be called by the familiar, Chris. Nor do I expect to be called Mr. Carter in my house. People know me by the name I use most commonly. That is the picture Moses was getting in this encounter with God. God was giving him the most familiar, commonly used names first, while reserving the names He uses least often for last.

Knowing Who God Really Is!

So what does that tell us? It shows that God wants humanity to know Him (and learn of Him) as the great I AM. Then, as God the Almighty. Then, He wants to show us His grace, compassion, patience, abundant love and truth, and endless capacity for kindness. The last parts of His name, the titles dealing with justice and sin, are just as legitimate and true to who He is. It's just that He wants us to be familiar with His goodness first.

Many Christians live every day in an unholy fear of God. It is a fear based more on condemnation than anything else. Instead of knowing God as the great I AM, who is so full of goodness, they just know Him as Mr. Judgment. And their actions reflect what they know and believe. They are bitter, unforgiving, and critical—all because they have learned about God the wrong way around. They know His judgment and His principals of divine retribution, and they believe these are the foremost aspects of His character. Such people live lives of fearful anticipation of God's hammer of judgment falling on them, which explains their usual lack of joy.

Most of us have lived at least a portion of our lives believing these same things. Getting acquainted with God's name is a good way to start correcting our bad theology. However, before we can take the next step, we have to stop and examine what we really believe. Are we ready to encounter the goodness of the Lord as it passes by? Are we done thinking of Him with a heart full of doubt and fear? Moses' encounter with God is a perfect model of what could happen when we say, "Lord, show us your glory!" God is going to start manifesting His goodness, sometimes in ways we might not be prepared for.

It could get overwhelming. It might alarm you. His gifts of glory have scared me silly on more than one occasion. Yet even when it takes me by surprise I keep coming back to Him for more. Even so, all this can be hindered by a lifetime of bad theology and bad habits if we don't deal with them first.

But if we allow the Lord's goodness to pass by in front of us, we might start to glow. Our bodies might start to transform like Moses' or Enoch's. Given that there is a generation coming that will know the glory (which is the same as the goodness) as intimately as Enoch did, I would think that Christians will be able to handle more and more of God's goodness, until all of it is passing by us on a daily basis. That last Christian generation will not just glow; they will translate into the glory.

Since that hasn't happened to me yet, the only course of action I know is to keep receiving His glorious goodness. I don't know how long it will be until we see Jesus returning in the clouds of Heaven, but sooner or later a generation will be prepared to walk in His glory as Enoch did.

Lessons about Goodness

When my daughter was only a few months old, she used to be so entertained by the smallest things. As a dad, when you see your kids give you a big smile and a giggle, you instantly hold on to whatever antic seemed to please them so that you can do it over and over again. For my daughter, the one that always got a great response was a gentle blow on her face, from me. The air would hit her round little cheeks and she would give me the biggest smile. So, naturally, I did it all the time because I enjoyed the response so much.

On one occasion, during a time of worship with the church, I was holding her in my arms and decided it was a good time to blow on her face again. Sure enough, out came that big, silly grin, and immediately the Lord started to speak to me. He said, "Why do you like to blow on her face?" I responded with, "Because I love the smile she gives me." Then the Lord said, "And how often do you like to do it?" I thought for a moment and said, "Probably seven or eight times a day."

Then came the lesson: "So if you like to blow on your daughter's face that often, just because you love the smile she gives you, how much do you think I would like to blow the Holy Spirit on your face just because I like the smile you give me?"

I have been told that God seldom asks us questions we know the answers to, but that He often asks questions to provoke us into new understandings. My first thought in response to this question—which I knew to be wrong but was honest nonetheless—was that He would want to blow on my face maybe once or twice in a day. I thought that for two different reasons. First, that's all I had really experienced up to that point in my life. All I was giving the Lord was one or two moments of undivided attention when He could pour out His blessings on me. So, in my ignorance, I assumed that was what God would want, too. The second reason is the far more destructive theology that thinks God would not want to pour out His Spirit on me multiple times during the day for no reason at all. But on the contrary, I now believe He wants to do that very thing because, like me, He just wants to see His kids smile.

Then, while I was still standing there holding my daughter, Luke 11:13 popped into my head:

If you then, being evil, know how to give good gifts to your chil-

dren, how much more will your heavenly Father give the Holy Spirit to those who ask Him?

Next came a repeat of the previous question, "How many times in a day do you think I would like to blow the Holy Spirit on you just because, when I do, you give me that wonderful smile?" Now I knew the right answer. He wants to pour out His Spirit on me far more than I want to bless my daughter. If I want to do that seven or eight times a day, He wants to bless me even more.

That seemed like a lot, but it was just the beginning of an understanding of how God desperately wants to fill us with His Spirit all the time. And the crazy part is that it is not even so we can go out and save the world. He just wants to blow the Spirit on us because we will give Him back a huge smile and heartfelt thanks. With God, everything is about a relationship with Him.

In my experience, posturing myself to receive God's Holy Spirit blessings did not come easily or naturally. It took some training. It took learning how to quiet my mind and get rid of all the thoughts that contradict how the Lord wants to grace me with His presence. And then, in the moments that I was directly aware of His Holy Spirit's movement, I also had to learn how to ignore and rebuff the other spiritual voices vying for access to my soul.

I believe, in order to start walking down the same road that Enoch traveled, we have to cultivate a life that allows for God's breath to hit us a dozen (or many more) times a day. We need a prayer life that lets God be as generous as He wants to be. If we can start to receive all of His good gifts, we will simultaneously be initiated into His glory. While I am sure it is a different process for everyone (and I don't believe there are three easy, "guaranteed" steps into the glory), I do think that practice makes perfect. So whatever you do, whether it is the exercises I am about to mention or your own, just do it with desperation.

Practice Receiving

The easiest way I know to make room for God's goodness in your life is through prayer. Most everyone has a typical prayer routine made up of requests, thanksgiving, and worship. Not many people give God the chance during their prayer time to dote on them as a Father would with His children, but this is a great first step into experiencing His goodness.

The next time you pray, block out about ten minutes in which you are completely silent before the Lord. During that time, ask the Lord to tell you how He feels about you. Just ask for it, and then start to listen. What will begin to come into your heart are some of the most powerful and encouraging words you will ever receive. You will be surprised how much God has wanted to tell you that He loves you and is proud of you. It might feel like a flood, only because His affection for you has been pent up for so long. If you have not given Him the opportunity to dote on you, it will feel like He is making up for lost time. Believe me, God does not want you to go through another day without giving Him the opportunity to pour out His love on you.

It sounds easy, yet many people find this extremely hard. If you don't think you deserve His adoration, then this will feel so unnatural that you will back out of it long before ten minutes have passed. Or, if you are convinced that the Holy Spirit won't speak to you, this exercise will be just as futile. If either of those are true, you must change what you think. If you can get over that hurdle, then it won't take long to see the difference. If you open that door just a crack, God will do the rest.

At first, I would physically recoil when the Lord would pour out His love and acceptance on me. He would start to tell me how He sees me and I would almost want to go hide, because—you guessed it—I didn't feel worthy. I also felt like I was a bad, lazy Christian just listening to the Lord speak good things to me. After all, weren't there starving people in Africa to go save? Surely there are churches to be planted in China. And yet, the word of the Lord was to sit and let Him love me. It is worth far more to Him to have one messenger fully equipped with His love, than a thousand who don't know the God they are serving.

For this exercise, it is important to listen very carefully. Take a look at this verse from Isaiah to see what I am talking about.

> *Listen carefully to Me, and eat what is good,*
> *And delight yourself in abundance. (Isaiah 55:2)*

If you find yourself starting to think about your sins or what you are doing wrong in life, stop! There will be plenty of time to recount all the things you feel you stink at. For now, just give God the chance to tell you encouraging and loving words. It's true that God can also express His love for you by revealing your sins, but there is a time for everything. At least for this exercise, try to stay focused on receiving His affection.

It will take a conscious effort to rule out the negativity, the concerns, and the religious tendency to be "productive" in prayer, and instead just listen to His good words. If you can block the other things out, you will find that you get delighted in His presence and abundance, as in the verse above. So, be encouraged to listen carefully; you may have to shut the door on some thoughts that are getting in the way of His doting affirmations.

The fact is that most people would be far more comfortable with a God who would focus on their sins than with the one who accepts them as they are. So, be prepared for your mind to make up lots of theological excuses about why this must be a dumb, even unspiritual pursuit. Then, after you have become good at receiving His love, look back and see if you still have a healthy respect for sin, or if you have become callous to purity and righteousness. I think you will find that getting flooded with His love will make you more attuned to what is pure and holy than ever before.

If you can get comfortable listening to His doting words, then you will likely experience a whole different interaction with the Lord in prayer. Letting His goodness in will start to open the door into more of His presence, and after you bask in that state for a while, start to envision some of the scripture verses that describe the access we have into the heavenly realm. Sometimes, using your God-given imagination to envision these concepts will go a long way toward further experiencing His presence. Here are some verses to get your imagination going:

> *But God, being rich in mercy, because of His great love with which He loved us, even when we were dead in our transgressions, made us alive together with Christ (by grace you have been saved), and raised us up with Him, and seated us with Him in the heavenly places in Christ Jesus. (Ephesians 2:4–6)*

> *Therefore let us draw near with confidence to the throne of grace, so that we may receive mercy and find grace to help in time of need. (Hebrews 4:16)*

> *He who overcomes, I will grant to him to sit down with Me on My throne, as I also overcame and sat down with My Father on His throne. (Revelations 3:21–22)*

For starters, just get a picture of Jesus in your head. Let Him look at you. Try to give yourself a chance to interact with the Holy Spirit. What does He look like? Is He doing anything? Next, watch His hands motion to you and then wave an invitation to come closer to Him. Accept His invitation and go closer. Feel the warmth in His countenance. He is always looking at you with warmth and adoration. Then, let Him show you the throne of God and watch Him as He sits down. Finally, see Him take you by your hand and bring you to the center of the throne and into an embrace with Him. Take your time with this visualization and try not to rush from one part to the next. If you can linger on each picture, a lot of detail will start to come into focus.

If given some time, these exercises can lead to all kinds of adventures with the Lord. Once you are in that receptive place and are surrendered to the Holy Spirit, you might start praying for something you don't know anything about. You might get a vision or start to sing a song you have never heard before. Again, the point isn't how you get to this place, just that you get there.

Another help is to focus your awareness on a certain scriptural principle. Push everything out of your mind and dwell on how accepted you are in God's sight. While you are praying, focus your thoughts and emotions on the constant welcome you have into God's presence. Think about how He will never turn you away, how you have full access into His throne room, how He longs for you to spend time with Him. Focusing on these truths can be enough to bring you to your knees, if you really believe them.

If you are wondering how to focus your mind, just think about what it feels like to worry about something. When you worry, all you can think about is whatever issue is eating at you that day. It turns your stomach and makes you testy because you can't let it go. Apply the same behavior to a scripture or spiritual exercise, and suddenly worry turns into meditation.

It is very empowering to believe that there is a standing welcome for you in the heavenly places. Not believing that truth will hinder every effort you make to get into His glory. When you know it's true, however, you start your prayer time with excitement and anticipation because you know anything can happen.

You are about to take Jesus' hand and be ushered up into a heavenly realm in which your interaction with the Father will seem otherworldly. Remember, prayer is supposed to be euphoric, and spending time with God feels better than anything else in the world. Practice letting Him dote on you until it becomes a daily experience.

Get Ready for a Ride

Sometimes these experiences are pleasantly peaceful, and other times you feel like you've been caught up in a Holy Spirit whirlwind that leaves you disheveled and a little wind-blown. There have also been plenty of times where God seems intent on doing spiritual surgery on you during prayer, and that can be an uncomfortable process. But regardless of the mood God is in, the result is always the same. You will end up wanting more of the Lord, feeling like you just tasted some of heaven's glory.

I had a whole season of my life during which, every time I prayed, the Lord would take me to some memory in the Spirit. I would start to see the memory as if I were watching myself from above. I would see the event take place as I remembered it, and then I would feel the presence of the Lord ask me to look for Him in the picture I was seeing. I would try to find Jesus in the memory, to see what He was doing while I was going through the same event. I would then see Him holding me while I made a horrible choice. I would see Him protecting me while a whole host of devils was attacking. I would even see Him correct the picture to show me that I wasn't remembering things the way they actually happened.

These journeys into the past were all taking place in the Spirit. It was the Lord's way of healing me of past hurts, by taking me back to when they happened and then showing me His grace and protection through it all. Those prayer times brought some much needed inner healing. If this is something you feel you need too, all you have to do is ask Him.

There were also times, when I was going through those memories, when I did doubt that what I was experiencing was real. I think it is normal, especially in our "modern" age, to question supernatural things, so it does take a sense of adventure to let go and see where the Holy Spirit will take you. For example, on one occasion the Lord was working on me to let go of my self-sufficiency and put my trust in His mercy. The Holy Spirit was taking me through the familiar pattern of revisiting memories to see where I picked up those bad behaviors. At the end of the process, when I felt like I had just fought (and lost) a twelve-round boxing match, the Holy Spirit said, "Would you like to test out your new freedom?"

Here is the point where you have to be ready to go on an adventure with the Lord. There is no telling what the Holy Spirit is going to say in these moments of close communion. My response to His question was cautious but willing. I said yes, but in a tone of voice that revealed I wasn't sure what I was getting myself into. The Lord then said, "You know I am preparing a place for you." I said, "Yes, Lord, I do." Then He said, "Would you like to see it?"

If I could get this moment back and redo it, I would have said, "Yes! Please show me!" But at the time, I was so dumbstruck by the invitation I could only say, "I don't know!" I look back at this moment all the time and laugh at myself, but that really was my best response in the moment. I didn't know if I wanted to see it because the freedom I was experiencing with the Lord was frightening. But, before my prayer breakdown was over, I did catch a tiny glimpse of the place God was preparing for me.

I saw a pure white gazebo with two chairs. The gazebo was sitting on the side of a hill full of lush green trees and foliage. And looking down the hill, past the gazebo, I could see the bluest, blue ocean. The scene was richer than anything I have ever witnessed on this planet. I knew when I saw this picture that the two chairs where there for me and the Lord, and I fully expect to talk with Him at that gazebo someday.

I am thankful that the Lord gave me a glimpse of that place before I jumped out of my skin and stopped praying altogether. He does realize these experiences are a stretch for us, but with each passing year we will get more and more accustomed to knowing Him in His Glory. That's why the importance of cultivating a prayer life that is full of His goodness cannot be overstated.

King David had some experiences just like the ones we have been talking about. In Psalm 36:7–9, David penned a beautiful, poetic picture of God's children basking in the glory.

How precious is Your lovingkindness, O God! And the chil-

dren of men take refuge in the shadow of Your wings. They drink their fill of the abundance of Your house; And You give them to drink of the river of Your delights. For with You is the fountain of life; In Your light we see light.

When you pray, are you drinking from the river of His delights? Are you drinking your fill from the abundance of His house? Would you call your prayer time "delightful?" The abundance is there for the taking, it just takes a believing heart to access it, and then prayer can be full of supernatural occurrences that leave you breathless.

He made that clear to me one evening while I was laid out on the bed, praying and enjoying His presence. I could feel that delightful river swirling around me, and I was suddenly tempted to get up and end the prayer time. I felt I had just checked off a box on my "to do" list. I wanted to spend some time in His goodness, and since that was happening, I was free to go about my business. Or so I thought.

Right before I got off the bed, the Lord said, "Don't run; stay." I had an impression that He would be disappointed if I got up now. He wanted more; He wanted me to go deeper. I stayed right where I was, struck in my heart by His love for me. As I stayed there, the presence got full and heavy. There was a weight on me that felt good. And the longer I stayed, the more His presence seemed to flood the room. Eventually, it got overwhelming, and with tears flowing down my face I said, "Lord, You have to increase my capacity to handle Your Presence, because it feels like You are going to burst me!" Truly, in that moment, I felt like all the atoms of my body were about to separate and be blown into the air.

Soon after, the heaviness and warmth subsided, and I was back to just lying on the bed. But I believe the cry of my heart is what He wanted to hear. He wants a people who will say, "Lord, increase our capacity to carry Your glory!" God will answer that prayer, but in the meantime, we can do our part, too. As I mentioned earlier, it doesn't matter what you do to build a knowledge of His goodness. Just do whatever it takes to open your heart to His delights, and do it diligently.

There will be plenty of time in the years to come to suffer for His name. There will be many times in your life when the Lord will lead you into intercession that doesn't feel good at all because it will be an invisible fight with unseen spiritual forces. And, there will be times when you approach the Lord with sorrow in your heart. That is all part of life.

Right now, however, we have grown so out of touch with this basic principle of His glory—that it is His good-ness—that we are missing out on a true experience of His presence. Let His goodness saturate you first, and then you will see that there is nothing in this world that can steal your joy.

5

RELEASING HIS GLORY

When I was a teenager, I developed a love for astronomy. I got hooked the first time I pointed a small, beat-up telescope at a random star only to find out it was, in fact, a planet and it had rings! It felt like I had discovered Saturn all over again— and from that moment on I never missed a chance to look up at the night sky.

As I studied physics and astronomy in college, the sheer size and scope of what I was looking at came into focus. Maybe the greatest benefit to my study of the cosmos was an understanding of how small we are compared to the vastness of God's creation. Yet, He chooses to place His Holy Spirit inside of tiny human hearts.

Years later, when I read the book of Joshua, one miracle in particular left me scratching my head because of its cosmic ramifications. The scene is the aftermath of a battle, and the Israelites are pursuing their enemies. Here is the account of what happens next:

> *Then Joshua spoke to the Lord in the day when the Lord delivered up the Amorites before the children of Israel, and he said in the sight of Israel:*

"Sun, stand still over Gibeon;
And Moon, in the Valley of Aijalon."
So the sun stood still,
And the moon stopped,
Till the people had revenge
Upon their enemies.

Is this not written in the Book of Jasher? So the sun stood still
in the midst of heaven, and did not hasten to go down for about
a whole day. And there has been no day like that, before it or
after it, that the Lord heeded the voice of a man; for the Lord
fought for Israel. (Joshua 10:12–14 NKJV)

When I read this passage, I can't help but wonder
what happened to the heavenly bodies to make them stand
still in the sky for a whole day. I think it is safe to assume that
our basic understanding of astronomy is accurate, and we
know from our primary education years that the earth re-
volves around its axis once every 24 hours, giving us the rising
and setting of the sun and the moon. Therefore, the physical
explanation is that the earth stopped rotating for about a day.
This is the only reason both the sun and the moon would
stop moving in their paths across the sky.

I know there are some fantastic miracles in the Bible,
but this has to be one of the most mind-boggling events on
record. It reminds me of Jesus' encouragement, "If you have
faith the size of a mustard seed, you will say to this mountain,
'Move from here to there,' and it will move; and nothing will
be impossible to you" (Matthew 17:20). I would love to know
how much faith it takes to say to the whole earth, "Stop mov-

ing!" What kind of man can make that prayer and the whole earth, all six septillion tons of it, obeys his command? (This is to say nothing of the forces involved in getting a six-septillion-ton object rotating at 1038 miles-per-hour to stop and start on a dime—but that's just the Physics talking.)

What Goes in Must Come Out

There is something in Joshua's life that might explain His extreme faith. Before he took the reins from Moses and began the conquest of the Promised Land, he was Moses' servant. Joshua learned about God as Moses' right hand man for many years, which means he experienced everything Moses did, right at his side. So, when Moses went to meet with the Lord, in those very same encounters in the glory that left him glowing, Joshua was there to observe and experience the same thing. There is no record of anyone else joining Moses in those intimate meetings inside the cloudy glory.

> *Whenever Moses entered the tent, the pillar of cloud would descend and stand at the entrance of the tent; and the Lord would speak with Moses. When all the people saw the pillar of cloud standing at the entrance of the tent, all the people would arise and worship, each at the entrance of his tent. Thus the Lord used to speak to Moses face to face, just as a man speaks to his friend. When Moses returned to the camp, his servant Joshua, the son of Nun, a young man, would not depart from the tent. (Exodus 33:9–11)*

It's the last part of that verse that should grab our attention. Joshua watched as God met with Moses face to face, and then, when Moses would leave, Joshua hung around for a while. This begs the question, "What happened after Moses left?" Did Joshua meet with the Lord in the same way? Did he just hang around in awe and soak up the residual presence? Was he just too in love with the Lord to leave no matter what happened? Joshua's actions tell us much about who he was. He wanted more of the glory, and he stayed because he loved God's presence. It is no wonder his prayers moved the earth.

It will be the same for us and for that last generation of Enochs as it was for Joshua. We have already seen how God desires this for all of His children. He wants us in His presence and experiencing His full glory more than anything. When the Lord spoke to me during my prayer time and said, "Don't run, stay," I felt the same invitation that I am sure Joshua experienced many times over. I thought it was time to leave, but God was saying, "Not yet, don't rush out of My Presence; learn to rest here." God is looking for people who will follow Joshua's lead and take experiencing His glory to the next level. He wants a church that will not depart from the tent but desire to just bask in His presence—even when everyone else has left and moved on.

Furthermore, there is a correlation between Joshua's hunger for God's presence and the power of his prayers. If you spend a lot of time in God's glory, eventually you reach a saturation point where it can't be kept inside any longer. And it's not that we are pursuing His glory so that we can have a supernatural ministry—it just happens this way naturally. It is only a matter of time until intimacy with God comes out as manifestations of His power.

Giving Freely

Since it is God's desire to unveil His glory to humanity, especially in these last days, it will be important for us to get ready to release all the goodness the Lord has poured into us. This part can be just as wild a ride as learning to receive from Him. I found that out for myself during a mission to Europe, not long after I began this journey into His goodness.

I was ministering with a friend of mine, and we were preaching to a church about how God is releasing His glory in these days. We spoke about healings and deliverances—even though to that date neither of us had witnessed a huge amount of miracles. But prior to that Sunday morning, we both had received visions that strengthened our faith for the impossible.

My friend had seen various pictures of demonic and occult activity and he figured we were going to encounter something of that nature when we ministered. I had seen a vision of someone committing suicide and, since I knew that it wasn't me, I also assumed it was for the next day's meeting. So, after we had given a quick word about God's outpouring of healing, we began to pray for the sick. We also made sure to give an invitation to anyone feeling suicidal, knowing full well that God had already promised to heal whoever might feel that way. At first, only a few people came forward for prayer; and then, before I could grasp what was happening, there was a line going out to the door of people needing a touch from the Lord.

The more we prayed, the more we could physically feel God's anointing. We prayed for all manner of sicknesses, injuries, and oppressions, and to us it seemed like no work at all. We just got to watch the Holy Spirit do miraculous things before our very eyes. A man who had cancer received prayer and spit out the tumor (he was later confirmed by a doctor to be cancer-free). Even his vocal cords, which had been destroyed by the cancer, were restored.

I saw people who suffered from depression become free from their illness instantaneously. I remember one lady being so free she literally danced away after prayer. A woman who was involved in the occult was totally delivered, and two people who were contemplating suicide were healed of the devil's lies. It was the most effortless and effective ministry I had ever experienced.

Over the course of three days, we ministered in what seemed like a mini-revival. In every meeting we prayed for the sick, imparted the Holy Spirit, and prophesied. I could sense a whole new freedom in the prophetic ministry. On more than one occasion, I would look at someone and I would instantly know their profession, what they were struggling with, and how they wanted God to work in their lives. Again, the effortlessness of receiving and delivering those words of knowledge and prophecy astounded me.

Meanwhile, throughout this whole experience, I kept thinking about everything the Lord had been telling me. He was intent on my learning to receive His glory, and now it was starting to come out without any work on my part. No struggle. No straining. No praying through gritted teeth while being half afraid that nothing was going to happen. The Holy Spirit did all the work, and we sat back and observed Him moving through us. It was delightful.

After that trip to Europe, I had a new understanding of the instructions Jesus gave to the Apostles before He sent them out to minister.

> *"And as you go, preach, saying, 'The kingdom of heaven is at hand.' Heal the sick, raise the dead, cleanse the lepers, cast out demons. Freely you received, freely give. (Matthew 10:7–9)*

If you have received freely, you should give freely. But, if you haven't received from Him, how can you give anything out? In other words, if you have been receiving from the Lord in your prayer time, as we have talked about, then you have been accepting His good gifts. You have been hearing His loving words. You have been allowing Him to dote on you. You have been receiving freely!

If you have rejected His efforts to love you, and if you resist His invitation to take you up into His presence, then you are not receiving from Him as He wills it. You have built up walls, be they theological or emotional, that keep you from this freedom. Consequently, when it comes time to minister in any capacity, you're just as bound in your giving as you are in your receiving.

I am inclined to think that many of our church inadequacies (which is a nice way of saying "our inability to live out the gospel") are due to our hindered and reluctant attitudes in receiving. If we could do the one right, it is only natural for the other to follow.

So, if you find yourself struggling to give out the message and demonstration of the gospel as Jesus instructed, do your personal inventory again. Is prayer a delight? Are you experiencing His presence? If not, then re-read chapters 1 through 5. You have to receive freely in order to give freely.

Faith in His Name

When I got back home from Europe, I was elated at what had happened; and I couldn't help patting myself on the back and saying, "Well done, Chris, you really did a good job receiving and releasing God's goodness." I think the Lord let me congratulate myself a little before He started to put things in perspective.

Even our best intentions to open ourselves up to God's goodness will never justify the miracles we will witness. As with the Laodicean church, He has determined to out-give us, not to reward us on a one-for-one basis for our own efforts. He knows that His unrestrained giving will push us further into intimacy with Him. So, we can all expect Him to do impossible things in our lives, even when we just barely grasp what His goodness is all about.

What we need is a good balance between two necessary understandings. First, comes the issue of receiving from Him in order to give His blessings to the world. Second, comes the truth that no level of effort on our part will make it happen. We have to stay dependant on His mercy, no matter how good we are at receiving His glory.

The book of Acts contains a great example of what the right perspective and balance looks like. It's the story of Peter and John going to the temple to pray and performing an impromptu healing at the temple gates. The man who was healed, a cripple from birth, went into the temple with them, leaping about and praising God. This is what happened next:

> *And all the people saw him walking and praising God; and they were taking note of him as being the one who used to sit at the Beautiful Gate of the temple to beg alms, and they were filled with wonder and amazement at what had happened to him.*

> *While he was clinging to Peter and John, all the people ran together to them at the so-called portico of Solomon, full of amazement. But when Peter saw this, he replied to the people, "Men of Israel, why are you amazed at this, or why do you gaze at us, as if by our own power or piety we had made him walk? The God of Abraham, Isaac and Jacob, the God of our fathers, has glorified His servant Jesus… And on the basis of faith in His name, it is the name of Jesus which has strengthened this man whom you see and know; and the faith which comes through Him has given him this perfect health in the presence of you all. (Acts 3:9–16)*

Peter struck the balance perfectly when he said, "Why are you amazed . . . as if by our own power or piety we had made him walk?" If there were any two men who might claim their godliness was sufficient, it could have been Peter and John. These were two seriously devout Apostles. But even so, they didn't think their pursuit of God or their commitment to Him had anything to do with the miracle. They give only two reasons for the man's healing: the name of Jesus and the faith that comes through Him. Think about that the next time God uses you. It is not your holiness, faithfulness, or effort that will cause the impossible to be possible. It is only faith in Jesus.

The same point is made in Jesus' response to a question proposed to Him after He miraculously fed five thousand people.

> *"What shall we do, so that we may work the works of God?" Jesus answered and said to them, "This is the work of God, that you believe in Him whom He has sent." (John 6:28–29)*

They asked Him a very human question. They just wanted to know what they had to *do*. Jesus' response is so un-religious it is almost painful. We don't have to do anything! We just have to believe. That takes all of the effort out of our hands and makes our sole responsibility a matter of faith.

It all comes down to what you believe. Specifically, that you believe in Jesus, not just in part but in all of Him. That means everything He said and everything He did. All the encounters with God I have shared in this book were examples of the Lord trying to show me who Jesus really is. Every one of those conversations was designed to correct my false assumptions and get me to really believe.

That doesn't mean I didn't believe in Him before, or

that I wasn't born again; it just means I wasn't believing fully and freely. I wasn't rejecting the Christian faith, but I was rejecting some of the crucial aspects of His character. That was the sole reason the Lord took me on a journey into His goodness and glory. It boils down to an issue of faith.

God knows that what we believe will always determine who we are and what we do, which is why He is taking great pains to get us to believe right. So what does all of this have to do with the balance I just mentioned? Well, if it isn't by our effort that the glory will come out, but it is only a matter of faith, then the way to get faith is through receiving from Him.

In other words, if you learn to receive freely, you will have faith in Jesus because you will know Him as He is. You will know Him fully. You will have remained in His glory long enough to know that He is all in all. That is what will build a glorious faith. If you can receive from Him, then you will know Him. If you know Him, then you will believe in Him. If you believe in Him, you will work the works of God.

That is how the glory was released through Peter and John that day in the temple. The power to heal came out of a deep intimacy with Jesus, but it still had nothing to do with their own efforts. And, by their own admission, it wasn't because they were godly men. The power was released because they believed.

Conversely, if you don't receive well, you probably don't feel like you know Him all that well either. And if you don't know Him, it is hard to truly believe Him. At that point, you are left with faith only in yourself. Most of us know that doesn't get us very far, and it certainly hinders any supernatural outpouring in our lives.

More Glory to Come

When we start to fully release God's glory, our Christian experience is going to look a lot like the book of Acts. Let's look at the passage when Philip preaches the gospel to Samaria to get an idea.

> *Therefore, those who had been scattered went about preaching the word. Philip went down to the city of Samaria and began proclaiming Christ to them. The crowds with one accord were giving attention to what was said by Philip, as they heard and saw the signs which he was performing. For in the case of many who had unclean spirits, they were coming out of them shouting with a loud voice; and many who had been paralyzed and lame were healed. So there was much rejoicing in that city. (Acts 8:4–8)*

The lame were healed, the oppressed were set free, and the city rejoiced. Can you imagine what it would take in our modern, intellectual age to get a whole city to rejoice? That will happen in our day if we can get back to preaching the good news of the gospel and letting God's brilliance shine through us.

Think for a minute about your own local setting. If you began healing those who were paralyzed, delivering people from mental illnesses, and giving people the best news they had ever heard, you might see much rejoicing in your city.

Philip brought the best news Samaria had ever heard, and he brought it out of the goodness he had received from the Lord. No one who has experienced God's glory will ever doubt that God wants to do good things for His children. They know that when God sends them to preach His gospel, He wants to bless everyone within hearing range in order to convince them that He is good. We don't have to question whether God wants to heal people. He does!

And that is just the beginning. The closer we come to that last generation of Enochs, the more we will experience this miraculous outpouring. Remember the first chapter in our discussion of the last days—it will be a time of such shaking and devastation that it will be allowed only once. But, in the midst of that turmoil, there will be a passionate group of Christians who have totally surrendered themselves to Jesus. They will be walking in the heavenly realms while they demonstrate the power of God to a suffering world.

Good News or Bad News

When you hear the good news of the Kingdom of God, your whole being comes alive. You feel empowered, loved, and convicted. The gospel will always make you want to run toward the Father, never away from Him. Sadly, at some point in our lives, most of us have heard the "bad news of the Kingdom."

I know I have heard it when someone presents a

form of gospel that is devoid of any demonstration of God's goodness. Sometimes it is a message of judgment, without any sense of salvation or restoration, and it never seems to bless anyone. I witnessed this while in college in South Carolina; one afternoon, a local minister came to our campus and began preaching on the street corner.

Now, before I go any further, let me say that I love it when inspired preachers take to the streets to proclaim the gospel. Doing so is Biblical and appropriate. However, on this specific day, the college campus got something less than inspired. From the beginning, I knew it was going to be a bust. The preacher started yelling at the people about all the sins he knew they were committing (which is okay), then moved on to telling them they were all going to hell (still okay—Jesus called people a "son of hell"), and finished up with... well... that was it.

Nothing about that message was new to me—I had heard similar preaching before. But there was something about his delivery that didn't sit right with me. It was so full of anger and bitterness that I felt it was worth a confrontation. I felt a sense of responsibility for my college campus, and I thought they deserved better.

I approached the man and asked him, "So, how many people have repented today? How many people have come to Christ?" His predictable response was "None." I did my best to communicate that no one was going to respond to a message that had already condemned them to hell, but it fell on deaf ears. He informed me that no preaching was correct unless it was about sin, righteousness, and judgment. All good Biblical principals from John, chapter 16, where Jesus described the work of the Holy Spirit.

So, it wasn't that this preacher was doctrinally wrong; he just wasn't full. What I mean is, he was preaching a form of the gospel out of his best intentions, but it amounted to just a small sliver of God's message to humanity. Plus, he didn't offer the slightest demonstration of God's power, just angry yelling.

To finish the story, I invited him to our campus meeting in the hope of coming to some kind of understanding. He said he would only come if we allowed him to preach, which confirmed what I thought in the first place. He wasn't interested in God's children, just his own misguided desire to yell at people. It was a classic case of someone ministering out of what he knew, and only that. If he had tasted the goodness of God, I imagine his heart would have been full of compassion, even if his message had still been about judgment.

The Bad Fruit

The story of that street preacher brings out a good point. Does our message always have to sound good, just because it's the good news? Will it always be a word that makes people happy? Does releasing God's glory always involve a smile on our faces?

To do that question justice we have to take a detour back to the garden. All of our thoughts about what is good and bad were established there, and it is important to make sure our definitions are the same as God's.

When Adam and Eve were created and given domin-
ion over the garden, they enjoyed an unhindered access to
God's presence. They could walk with Him and talk with Him
without any barriers. Also, all they knew was what God told
them, and everything He told them was good. The problem
came when they ate the forbidden fruit.

> *Now the serpent was more crafty than any beast of the field
> which the Lord God had made. And he said to the woman,
> "Indeed, has God said, 'You shall not eat from any tree of the
> garden'?" The woman said to the serpent, "From the fruit of
> the trees of the garden we may eat; but from the fruit of the
> tree which is in the middle of the garden, God has said, 'You
> shall not eat from it or touch it, or you will die.' " The serpent
> said to the woman, "You surely will not die! For God knows
> that in the day you eat from it your eyes will be opened, and you
> will be like God, knowing good and evil." When the woman
> saw that the tree was good for food, and that it was a delight to
> the eyes, and that the tree was desirable to make one wise, she
> took from its fruit and ate; and she gave also to her husband
> with her, and he ate. Then the eyes of both of them were
> opened, and they knew that they were naked; and they sewed
> fig leaves together and made themselves loin coverings. (Genesis
> 3:1–7)*

The tree of the knowledge of good and evil was off
limits, and the consequences of their sin and their motivation for committing it are played out through the entire Bible.
There is a lot more to this passage than we can dissect here,

but one issue in particular is worth looking at.

Up to this point, Adam and Eve believed every word that came out of God's mouth to be righteous, truthful, and good. The devil planted a lie in Eve's head, and that was the first lie humanity ever believed. Here is the lie:

What God has said isn't the best thing for you.

Every hardship and every injustice in our world can be attributed to that same prodigious lie. All of the "intelligent" denials of God's truth that are so rampant today come from this source. That original lie represents a rejection of what God has said because of a belief that His words are bad.

It is easy to see why humanity is in the mess it is in. For every issue in life, there is something in the scriptures to guide us; and if we would just agree that what it written is good, then all our problems would vanish. But in all institutions of our modern world, from government to nutrition, we can see how man has decided God's word is bad and has chosen a different way. Hence, the horrible state of the world.

That lie set Adam and Eve on the wrong path, and the fruit sealed the deal. Once they'd eaten the fruit, their eyes were opened and they could know both good and evil. And now that they knew evil as well as good, they could judge between the two—even if they did so poorly. So, from that day on, mankind has been judging whether what God says is good or bad.

Many believers aren't aware of how much they judge God's words. It happens when the Lord is telling them to talk to a stranger about the gospel, or pray for a sick neighbor, and they decide on their own that the best plan is to do nothing. In that moment, they have decided for themselves that what God said was not the best thing for them. They probably thought more about ridicule or their own embarrassment. They weighed the consequences of their actions verses the potential benefits. And, the end result was to do exactly the opposite of what God commanded.

Years ago, my wife and I felt called to move into a bad neighborhood. We knew it was risky, but at least on this occasion we didn't judge God's word. We moved in and experienced life in a high-crime part of town. We experienced break-ins, vandalism, drive by shootings, and drug busts right next door. And through it all, we never regretted the decision to move in. It was, without a doubt, the best place we could be.

God changed us in that neighborhood. He gave us a heart for the poor and showed us His protection. We never got scared (okay, maybe once or twice) and we were pushed into a deeper relationship with Him. We would not be who we are today without that experience, yet the tendency to judge God's commands still hinders us. When we feel the Lord asking us to take a mission trip, or when we feel Him telling us to give extra money, we still have this reluctance to immediately obey.

But there is a way to get that fruit out of our lives. The more we conform ourselves to Jesus, the more that knowledge is purged out of our spirit. Eventually, we will find ourselves looking at the Lord and saying, "Everything you say is good!" It will feel like we are back in the Garden of Eden.

When Good Seems Bad... But Is Still Good

When Jesus preached, He didn't always say nice things. If the people had the wrong heart they might have been offended and written Him off as a false Messiah, and some did just that. One woman, however, had every reason to get mad but somehow kept her cool. Let's look at her story.

> And a Canaanite woman from that region came out and began to cry out, saying, "Have mercy on me, Lord, Son of David; my daughter is cruelly demon-possessed." But He did not answer her a word. And His disciples came and implored Him, saying, "Send her away, because she keeps shouting at us." But He answered and said, "I was sent only to the lost sheep of the house of Israel." But she came and began to bow down before Him, saying, "Lord, help me!" And He answered and said, "It is not good to take the children's bread and throw it to the dogs." But she said, "Yes, Lord; but even the dogs feed on the crumbs which fall from their masters' table." Then Jesus said to her, "O woman, your faith is great; it shall be done for you as you wish." And her daughter was healed at once. (Matthew 15:22–28)

This doesn't sound like a "nice" Jesus at all. At first He doesn't even answer her, and then He insults her. What would you do if Jesus implied that you were a little dog? Would you still want Him praying for your daughter? If I am being honest, I might have responded with a sarcastic jab and then told Him He could keep His Kingdom to Himself. Here she is begging for help and He gives her this harsh response.

But, that isn't the end of the story. This was a special lady, and you can argue that her desperation led her to overlook His comment, but I think something else was at work. When He implied that she wasn't worth His attention, she didn't get mad because she didn't judge what He said to be good or bad. On the contrary, when she heard His words she knew they were coming from the Messiah. She was thinking, "This is God in the flesh!" She called him "Lord" and "Son of David." There is no mistaking that she knew who she was talking to. It didn't matter to this woman what He said because, to her, everything He said was good! He was the Messiah. He could do no wrong.

In the face of a response that many of us would have instantly judged to be prideful and haughty, she said, "Yes, Lord." She instantly agreed with His assessment. How could she say that if not for a refusal in her mind to try to judge God's words? For that moment, she was back in the garden and everything that God said was the best thing for her. I have often thought that she said in her heart, "Jesus, You are the Messiah. Everything You say is good and I know You love me beyond measure. If You say that I am a dog, then that is exactly what I am, and it is good."

The story ends happily. Her daughter is healed and she receives a compliment rarely given in Jesus' ministry. He affirms her great faith, which was ultimately a faith in Jesus, just as we have been talking about.

Now let's make a quick leap back to that Enoch generation. That last batch of Christians will be experiencing God's goodness on such an unprecedented level because they believe Him to be only good. They, too, will have regurgitated the fruit of the knowledge of good and evil and will be right back where man started, with a singular understanding of His goodness. That, more than anything, is what allows them to walk in the heavenly realms and demonstrate the gospel to a fallen world. Getting back to our question, though, when the good news comes out, does it always sound good?

If we are anything like the Christians of the Bible, then there will be times when the goodness of God will come out as a stern portent of judgment. The message might be full of fiery conviction that leaves us feeling a little timid. But, if we imitate our Lord, then even the harshest messages will be coupled with an outpouring of love and miracles. People will know that even when God says something difficult to receive, it is still good.

Jesus was famous for giving the harshest rebukes and then going off to heal an entire town full of sick people. He could unerringly walk the line between telling the truth to a sinful world and demonstrating God's abundant love. And that is another defining characteristic of the last Christian generation. They will be confronting the world in the worst spiritual and moral shape it will ever know. And, like Jesus, they will have to give it a message of divine rebuke and correction—even while they are healing crippling diseases and cancers. Their hearts will be moved with compassion as they give God's final plea to mankind.

That should be our goal. No matter what the message is, whether it is an intense correction or a gentle encouragement, it should be coupled with a release of His glory.

6

THE OPPOSITION

I had a dream one night that began with me playing in a river. Other people I knew were there as well, and we were all swimming and paddling around in small boats. The river was in the middle of a green valley and at the mouth of the river stood a large, palatial house. The house was white and perched on top of a hill overlooking the source of the river. Leading up the hill were sets of steps and terraces—a flight of steps, then a terrace, another flight, then a terrace, and so on.

At the top, inside the house, I could see other brothers and sisters in the Lord. It was the start of a new day and everyone was preparing to go out and play in the river. At that point, my father appeared and told me he had made breakfast for everyone. I responded to him that everyone had already made their own breakfasts and were getting ready to leave.

He seemed disappointed, and I started to wonder in the dream if this really was my father or if it was my *Father*. I went out to one of the terraces where I knew He had prepared breakfast and I saw a long table set with cream-colored alabaster jars and plates. The only food I could see on that simple table was the elements of the Lord's supper.

At that point, I knew it was my heavenly Father who

was speaking to me, and the meal He had prepared for every-one was communion. As soon as I realized this, I began to fly from the house down the river. As I flew, the sky grew very dark and ominous, with black and green clouds rolling in. I flew all the way to the point in the river where we were play-ing at the beginning of the dream. Only now the river was completely dried up and all the boats we had been using were beached on a dry riverbed.

There was one boat still moving among all those which had been abandoned. It looked like an ancient Egyp-tian river boat, like something a pharaoh would be depicted in, sailing the Nile River. Inside that boat was a man and a group of servants. The man was dressed like an Arab sheik, and while I was still watching, one of the servants told me the sheik's name was Hitler's Lamb.

The Coming Battle

Now, before we tackle the sheik in the boat, let's look at the first part of the dream. At the beginning, when we were playing in the river and milling about the Father's house, we were missing the blessing He had prepared for us. That communion table telegraphed one of the most important messages of the whole dream. While it is certainly good to be in the house of the Lord and to be experiencing His river, He wanted to draw His children in to a close communion. He wanted to feed them His body and His blood; but, sadly, everyone had already fed themselves.

The implications of this are clear. Today, there are Christians who have missed a deep, intimate relationship with the Lord because they are self-sufficient. They are too busy living life on their own, and therefore they pass up numerous chances to interact with God. They might have come to faith in Jesus and go to church, but they are uninterested in delving deeper into Jesus. They are in the Lord's house, but they are not eating at His table.

Going back to the dream, I won't forget the sense of disappointment on the Father's face as His children passed up the chance to get into His presence. Furthermore, God knew what was coming. He let me fly back down the river to see the storm clouds gathering and the river drying up, to show me why His breakfast invitation was so important. The Lord knows that the spiritual climate in the whole world is going to become hostile. He has also shown us in the scriptures (we will visit some of these scriptures later) that many believers will lose their faith or be deceived.

The invitation to have communion with Him was just as much a reflection of His desire to know us as it was a preparation. God knows the only thing that will steady us when the sky gets sinister and the river dries up is a deep connection to Him. If we have taken the time to get close to Him, then no future darkness will separate us.

The river in this dream was a symbol of our current Christian experiences. It is our church life as we know it right now, and the Lord is saying that it is about to dry up. That doesn't mean there won't be any churches or expressions of Christianity; it just means the way we do it is about to drastically change. To be specific, the dark clouds and dry riverbed are a picture of persecution and apostasy (falling away from the faith). The persecution will come as the world gets further away from God's truth and ultimately gives in to its hatred of God, and the apostasy will come as the mainstream church falls deeper and deeper into unbelief and false doctrines. Eventually, what the world acknowledges as "the church" will be nothing more than a dry, empty riverbed.

But, those who know their God and have come to eat at His table will be flying above it all. That doesn't mean we won't experience the persecution, but it does show us that we won't lack for a Christian experience. In fact, our church life in those days will be more filled with His glory than at any point in history.

We don't know when the world climate is going to change; and not being ready could prove disastrous, so the important thing is to get to know Him in His glory right now. That is the only foolproof way to not get stuck in the dry river bed, especially since something very bad is going to be roaming around.

Who Is Hitler's Lamb?

And that brings us to the sheik. The significance of his Arabic dress and Arabic boat was not lost on me, but that is a discussion for another book. For now, let's just look at his name—Hitler's Lamb.

Jesus was the only person to have a title that included the word Lamb, so right off the bat we are dealing with a person who wants to be like Jesus, the Lamb of God. Only he isn't the lamb of someone holy, he is the lamb of Hitler. So, he is a man who wants to be like Jesus and is also a representation of all the hideous and evil things Adolph Hitler brought on this earth. Sounds a lot like the classic picture of the Antichrist. He is the successor to the same Antichrist government that the world witnessed in Nazi Germany, and he is going to make his entrance soon. Also, his boat was the only vessel that could still move around that dry riverbed, which means he will supplant every other religious experience in that day.

So, the message is simple. The river that we are all freely playing in will one day be replaced with an empty, Antichrist system, and the only believers who won't get sucked in will be those who have sat down to have communion with Jesus. There is no getting around it—the believers of the last days will have to deal with the Antichrist.

You can see the stage being set. On one side there is the rise of the Antichrist over an apostate church, and on the other side is a group of last days Christians who are glowing with His glory. Lest we be fooled, the devil knows what the last Christians are capable of, and he does not want the world to see God's glory at a time when he is trying to drag everyone to hell.

At the time of this writing, the riverbed hasn't dried up (although it may be starting to) and Hitler's Lamb is not walking the earth; but the devil is just as motivated to hinder God's children from experiencing His glory. His goal right now is to stop that last generation of Enochs from emerging at all.

That is the fight we are in right now. God is calling us to step into His presence, and the devil is trying to keep us out. He's pushing and promoting a whole hellish strategy to keep believers out of the glory and in the status quo. The dream about the Antichrist was a great warning of what is to come, but there is also a very real battle raging at this very moment. We have to look at the spiritual powers that are trying their best to keep us out of God's goodness. Although it isn't always fun to dissect the devil's strategy, we can take encouragement in knowing that everything he does always backfires and fulfills God's purposes. Whether he likes it or not, there is a generation of Christians who will be waiting for Christ's return. And they will be full of God's glory.

My Personal Fight

The best way I know of to describe what the devil is trying to do is to give my own personal experience with his lies, and I don't think my story is unique. I would imagine that many people have experienced a similar pattern, even if the details are a little different.

Like many Americans, I was raised in a Christian home and was brought to church on a regular basis. I was baptized at eleven years of age, and that really was the moment I knew that I needed Jesus. I had a rebellious adolescence, and before I graduated high school I felt convicted and rededicated my life to the Lord. I left for college with every intention of living out my faith and staying focused on

God's desire for my life, and I was going along just fine until the beginning of my junior year. At that time, and without any prompting of my own, the Lord decided to introduce me to His Holy Spirit. That was the end of my Christian life as I knew it.

Prior to that moment, if anyone asked me, "How does God speak?" I would have said, "You read your Bible and pray, and somehow in that process you know what to do." After the introduction into His Spirit, I said, "He just speaks! Sometimes audibly!" And that was the truth. My whole interaction with the Lord changed almost overnight, and I found myself on a rollercoaster ride with the Spirit.

For the first time in my life, I experienced visions— both when I was awake and asleep. I saw miracles for the first time. I was devouring the scriptures as if I couldn't get enough of the Word. On one occasion, the Lord called my name audibly and I just froze right where I was. I felt closer to the Lord than ever before, and I loved it. It was a complete transformation of my understanding and relationship with God, and it felt like I had finally come alive. For six months of my junior year, from November to April, I was flying high on the wind of the Holy Spirit and discovering something new every day.

What happened at the end of those six months is the reason this story fits into the chapter called "The Opposition." It is a picture of the lengths to which the devil will go to get you out of God's abundance. I knew something was wrong when I woke up one morning in April. I had been wrestling the previous night with my own sinful desires, and some demonic activity as well, so I didn't get much sleep. But when I woke up, I felt so bad that I knew it could not even be blamed on the previous night's unrest. I just felt horrible— even depressed. I cried and grieved and spent a whole day just wandering around my apartment, aimlessly. I would walk into a room and not even know why I was there, or I just laid on my bed staring at the ceiling, wondering what was wrong.

For six months prior to that day, I had felt like I was standing under a fully opened fire hydrant of the Holy Spirit; but as of that morning, the flow was completely turned off. And that was the worst feeling imaginable. It was like going from the most intimate and powerful interaction I had ever had with the Lord to feeling like I didn't know Him at all.

Does God Ever Forget Us?

If God were not omniscient, I would have sworn He had forgotten I existed. And there was no distinction between what I knew to be doctrinally true and how I felt. In other words, I knew God would never leave me, but I felt so abandoned it didn't even matter. To people around me, it looked as if I'd had a mental breakdown. Some even suggested I seek professional help. But, as awful as I felt, I still believed it was a spiritual issue.

That was the start of a long season of feeling like God didn't want to talk to me or interact with me at all. For the better part of three years I lived in a state of disappointment and sadness. I felt like I had lost the greatest thing that ever happened to me—an unhindered relationship with God.

I became really good at expressing my anger to God in prayer. It didn't phase me to throw my Bible against the wall and yell at the Lord, because in my mind an angry God was better than no God at all. It was misguided I know—but I was trying to make Him mad so that He would at least acknowledge me.

Over time, the anger subsided and I learned to be at peace with something less than what I had experienced during those six months in college. I felt an obligation to come to terms with it and even embrace it, because I was convinced God had ordained that season. I told myself it was a wilderness experience, or what some people have called "the dark night of the soul." I rationalized that God wanted me in this place of silence and frustration so that I would learn to trust Him more, and that was true—just not in the way I thought.

After the first three years, which was the worst of it by far, I started to regain some ground and was living relatively free and happy. I was enjoying ministering in every capacity in which God led me, and felt like I was hearing His voice clearly and frequently. And I didn't think much about that April morning anymore, because my relationship with the Lord was active and growing.

About eleven years after the beginning of that dark season, long after I had come to terms with it, the Lord brought it back up. It surfaced again when the Lord started to introduce me to His goodness. As you might remember from the first chapter, I mentioned fighting a battle in my head when God would start to pour out His abundance on me. Well, this is the rest of that story.

Remembering the Darkness

From the very first instance of God showering me with His abundance and love, I would feel a hesitation to receive it. And, when I would pray, it felt like I was hitting a wall over and over again. Furthermore, when I would finally receive what God was giving, I had this nagging thought that I was doing this all wrong and God was upset with me. Eventually, I got frustrated enough to fast and ask God what was going on, and that's when the past started to resurface. As I mentioned before, God can take you back through memories to heal you of past hurts and failures.

I remembered how good it felt to be so close to Him in college, and I also saw how awful it was when it all crumbled several months later. But I started to hone in on a feeling as I revisited these memories. I felt hurt. I felt like God had hurt me. So, here I was trying to grab hold of His abundance, but feeling like God hurt me eleven years earlier. And when the Lord asked me to honestly tell Him what I was feeling, it came out in the statement, "Lord, I want to trust you, I really do, but I am afraid you are going to hurt me again."

It was such a release to be honest. I felt like God had taken away the greatest thing that ever happened to me, and now I wasn't sure if I could trust Him. If I was going to receive His new blessing, which seemed just as good if not better than what I had experienced in college, what guarantee did I have that He wouldn't take this away, too?

What happened next was the start of the healing process. I was seeing the memory of that horrible April morning from above, watching myself pace around my apartment like a lost man. I saw myself grieving, and then I heard the Lord say to me, "Where am I in this picture?"

I was expecting to see God leaving or casting me away into a desert. But what I saw was Jesus holding me, and then the whole picture changed as I began to see a dark force attacking me, over and over. I was amazed as I watched this, because I was so sure it was the Lord who had made me feel so bad. Now I was seeing the real source of the oppression, and in the midst of that picture I heard the words, "I wasn't the one who hurt you."

I was stunned. For eleven years I had been convinced God was teaching me some lesson about hardship, and now I was seeing the past as it had really happened. I saw the darkest, most vile presence biting and clawing at me as I walked around my apartment in depression. Thank God for Jesus' sustaining hold on me or who knows what could have happened.

I stayed in that moment in prayer for a long time, just thinking about the words, "I wasn't the one who hurt you." I could feel my heart start to let in more of God's goodness as I let go of the hurt. The more I would give the pain to Him, the more I would feel a release in the Spirit. It felt so good to know that God hadn't hurt me, and I was making my first steps back toward trusting Him, but it wasn't over yet.

I knew everything hadn't been resolved because I kept thinking, "The only way the devil could hurt me is if God didn't protect me." So, it seemed to me that the Lord was still responsible. If He allowed it to happen, then wasn't He the one to blame for the whole ordeal? I started to get mad at

Him again, this time for letting it happen. I agreed that He didn't attack me, but where was the protection? Where was the warning? From that point forward, God began to teach me some truths that get right to the core of life. So, even if it seems like a stretch, hang in here for the whole story.

I was trying to wrap my mind around a basic issue. If I deserved to be protected, and God didn't protect me, then God must be unjust. Since we know that isn't true, something else had to be at work here. So, I knew He didn't protect me from the devil's attack. He was with me and sustained me, but He didn't stop it from happening. And, at the same time, I knew God was perfect—so the only solution could be that I didn't deserve protection.

Now, before you say, "Of course you deserved protection! God loves you and would never leave you unprotected," just wait to hear the rest of the story. I had to come to terms with this in order to continue the healing process. The truth I had to agree with was this: I did not deserve anything good from Him. Once that realization set in, I heard the Lord say, "Did you deserve for me to pour out my Holy Spirit on you in college?" "No," I responded. And that was the truth. I didn't deserve to have my life radically changed. God did it on His own initiative; I didn't even know to ask for it.

Then, the Lord put the two ideas together for me. He showed me that I didn't deserve to be blessed in the first place, and I didn't deserve to be protected from the loss of that same blessing. I thought about it, and then in a moment of frustration yelled out, "So what does that mean—that I'm just at your mercy?" It was as if all of Heaven looked down on me and quietly said, "Yes."

And then I realized what I had said. I meant it as a frustrated jab at the Lord, like I was insinuating that He didn't care and we were all just at His whim. But God used the words I said in anger to speak the deepest truth into my heart. I was living, breathing, and relating to Him because of His mercy.

Seeing the Picture Clearly

You know when you've hit a breakthrough because you feel like you just reached the summit of Mt. Everest and it's all down hill from there. Once I realized everything was an issue of God's mercy, all sorts of things came into perspective. The Lord told me that He wanted that season of glory in college to last forever. But, the only way to make it last a lifetime was to deal with my own bad beliefs and behaviors. He told me that if He hadn't let the devil attack me, than I would have gone my whole life thinking that I was responsible for this Holy Spirit outpouring. I would have believed He blessed me because I was worthy. That would have eventually killed any move of His Spirit.

Instead, God knew I needed to understand mercy, and that the only way to sustain a move of the Holy Spirit that powerful was to get me eternally connected to His goodness. I had to be forever dependant on Him.

He also let me in on the devil's plan too. He showed me how the Kingdom of God was advancing so strongly at the college that it got hell's attention. I was one of many students who experienced the revival, and the campus was alive with passionate believers in unity. So, the devil took six months to plan an assault and then opened fire. Needless to say, I wasn't the only one who felt crushed that April morning.

When I began to see the background of what had happened to me, I also caught on to another reason for the whole event. The Lord wanted me to come face-to-face with my adversary. He wanted me to see the lies so that I would know what I was up against. The lies that I faced were specially crafted to derail a whole generation of believers; in just a moment, we will look at exactly what the devil did to keep me out of God's goodness.

But first, to finish this story, the last point God made to me that day started with this fundamental awareness. If everything God gives me is an act of His mercy, and not a response to anything I deserve, then who can take away the good gifts of God? I was free to receive everything He was offering me without fear—because I knew He was giving them to me freely and without cost. He was giving me gifts of mercy. Finally, I heard the Lord say to me, "I didn't hurt you." That sentence brought me full circle, and I remembered what He had told me at the start of that healing time. Where at first He said, "I wasn't the one who hurt you," now He was saying that I was never even hurt.

What God allowed to happen didn't hurt me, and that may be the most stunning truth of all. The most painful and traumatic event of my life brought me to a deep connection with Jesus and allowed me to receive more of His heart into mine. The devil's entire strategy ended up connecting me to more of God's power, which must have really frustrated hell. It almost made me laugh that the devil had worked for eleven years on something that did the exact opposite of what was intended.

In the hands of the Lord, the darkest moments in our lives will be used to fashion us into His image. And, the more you are "in His image," the more you will experience the power and blessing of God. So, if the devil's best-laid plans only serve to bless us, why would any of us have a hard time trusting Jesus? With Him, we never suffer loss.

A Deceptive Voice

Most Christians expect to be able to identify the Antichrist (or, at least those who think they will still be on the earth) when he arrives. We expect him to be like Hitler, a world leader who functions like evil personified. We expect something supremely vile that will persecute us and demand worship. To be fair, the Antichrist will be all those things; but he isn't just the polar opposite of Jesus Christ. For at least a portion of his reign, he will look so much like Jesus it will deceive many, many people. Here is where we need a good definition of Antichrist. It doesn't just mean "opposite of Jesus," it can also mean "pretending to be like Jesus."

Maybe the greatest deception of the last days will be the emergence of a ruler who appears to be so Christlike that people will give him the worship he craves even before he demands it. He will look and act like a savior, and he will know how to mimic Jesus' voice perfectly. More than anything, the Antichrist will be an accomplished actor parading up and down on a worldwide stage.

When I woke up that morning in April, I started hearing a lying voice, and I was convinced it was God's. It was saying to me, "You really enjoyed my presence didn't you? Now I have to teach you how to live without me so you can be a strong believer. You are going to live in silence for a while, until you get stronger." I was receiving all of it because I didn't know I could hear a voice other than the Father's. And underneath these words of separation was the smallest touch of disappointment. As a result, I had a nagging feeling that God was leaving me because I wasn't good enough.

However, that feeling of condemnation was so small in comparison to the "fatherly" words about endurance and toughness. Can you see the set-up? A spirit came to me that morning, and he knew how to mimic God's voice so effectively that I was instantly deceived. It sounded so much like the Father, even though it felt so bad. I was a young and immature believer, and I didn't know any better. So, I took in the devil's lies and believed God had left me.

You might be reading this and thinking, "Of course it was the devil, Chris. God would never make you feel that way. Why didn't you realize that wasn't Him?" The answer is that I believed him because the deception was so strong—and that brings me to a serious warning. The strength of the deception to be unleashed on believers in the last days will be unparalleled, and it will be far easier than any of us want to think to call something holy when it is really profane. Someone is going to emerge who will appear to be so much like Jesus that even solid Christians will be tempted to worship him. Here is the forewarning straight from Jesus, Himself:

> "Then if anyone says to you, 'Behold, here is the Christ,' or 'There He is,' do not believe him. For false Christs and false prophets will arise and will show great signs and wonders, so as to mislead, if possible, even the elect. "Behold, I have told you in advance. (Matthew 24:23-26)

And again in 2 Thessalonians:

> The coming of the lawless one is according to the working of Satan, with all power, signs, and lying wonders, and with all unrighteous deception among those who perish, because they did not receive the love of the truth, that they might be saved. (2 Thessalonians 2:9–10 NKJV)

The devil has had a long time to practice mimicking God's voice. Even in the Garden of Eden he spoke to Eve in words that, to her, weren't obviously anti-God. He told her something that sounded wise, and she believed it.

As for me, I spent eleven years believing that God had hurt me; and on top of that, I believed I was supposed to be okay with it all. It sounded right enough. I reasoned that God needed me to go without His presence so I could get tougher and be a better servant. But, the lies that sounded so reasonable were intended to build up and feed into my distrust of God. *God hurt you... so you can't trust Him.*

All of it was to keep me out of His glory. And, more specifically, to stop me from experiencing His glory while I was in college. Thank the Lord it didn't work! But, the way the devil tried to sneak in, with that smooth, lying voice, is the characteristic way he tries to separate everyone from God's goodness.

Seeing the Antichrist Spirit

As mentioned before, the last generation of Christians will have to deal with the Antichrist, and even today there is a similar battle raging. We can't afford to stick our heads in a hole and pretend there aren't dark spiritual powers in the air above us, trying to keep us from fullness in Christ. If we need more proof, listen to what the Apostle John said to the church.

> *... and every spirit that does not confess Jesus is not from God; this is the spirit of the Antichrist, of which you have heard that it is coming, and now it is already in the world. (1 John 4:3–4)*

There will absolutely be an incarnation of the Antichrist on this earth. The Bible refers to him as the "man of sin" or "man of lawlessness." Meanwhile, there is also a spirit, a powerful fallen angel, who has taken the same job. It is the Antichrist spirit, and he exists solely to mimic Jesus and thus deceive many. When you see a story in the news of a person doing something heinous because "God told them to do it," you have just seen the Antichrist spirit at work. That is the most extreme example, but we might be shocked to learn how much that fallen angel is working all around us.

If you can imagine a version of Jesus that appears to be ninety-nine percent true but is one percent lie, then you get a good picture of this spirit. It doesn't want to give itself away as an imitation; rather, it wants to act like the real thing so we are tempted to listen to it. To be specific, it wants people to go to church. It wants people to pray and read their Bibles. It has no problem with mission trips, tithing, and worship services. That is all part of the "truth" it presents. Its goal isn't to get you worshiping idols and practicing voodoo; its method is far too subtle for that.

What it does want is for all Christians to keep going to church without ever realizing how much God adores them and longs to give to them. It wants the relationship going only one way—us to God. You can see it everywhere. Worship services are conducted and the people give God songs and money and they sit and listen to a sermon, but they have not entered into His heavens and received one thing from the riches of His glory.

The Antichrist spirit has effectively injected the one percent lie: God is good, *but not so good* as to shower you with His glory. So, when we come to worship, we keep giving and giving to God in a subconscious effort to appease Him, when all God really wants to do is spend time with His kids. To put it simply, the Antichrist spirit wants a person to think of God as a loving, wise presence that saved them from hell yet is eternally unreachable. Can you see the craftiness of the lie and how it is calculated to keep us out of the Lord's glory?

When my eyes were opened to what had been deceiving me all those years, and how it had kept me from receiving God's goodness, I could immediately see how it has also affected the whole Christian experience for many others. However, that doesn't mean that everyone going to church is under some demonic influence and isn't born again; it just means we need to be aware of what the devil is trying to do. This isn't an issue of salvation; it's an issue of fullness and glory. Everyone has problems because of the lies they believe; sadly, that's part of being a human. The fun part comes when God starts revealing what the lies are and we begin getting free. And for the church in America, it is time we knew what has been holding us back.

If you are wondering how we can know where this spirit is working, just look at the places where Jesus is accepted. Remember, it's the Antichrist spirit and not the anti-Buddha spirit. Therefore, the places that are most open to Christianity are the same countries in which this spirit has taken up residence. Since a fallen angel cannot be omnipresent, I would think his home would be in the nation most known for an acceptance of the gospel.

If we wanted to test that theory, then the nation that spirit has called home should be full of churches but lacking in true belief. We should expect to see a lot of people claiming to be born again but not behaving in any discernable Christlike way. That nation would be a nation of believers stuck in ruts and not experiencing God's glory.

Encouragement to Fight

What I experienced in my own life, and what is happening all over the world, is a showdown between two entities. On one side is an emerging group of people who are desperate for God's glory, and on the other is the spirit of the Antichrist. One is preparing to commission Jesus in the earth like never before, and the other is trying to spread a version of Jesus tainted with lies.

It is a tough battle to be sure, and we might need a little encouragement to believe the final outcome will be in our favor. For me, that confirmation came from an unlikely place. Indeed, if you come from a protestant background you will understand why I say "unlikely." Growing up, I read a Bible with sixty-six books in it, but Catholic and Orthodox Christians have a Bible that includes another fourteen books, called the Apocrypha.

One night I had a dream in which the Lord showed me a gold book sitting on a huge stone table. The front cover of the book, which depicted a beautiful bride, said the story was from the book of Judith in the Apocrypha. At that moment, I had no knowledge that book existed, but the dream seemed pretty specific. As soon as I could, I got my hands on a Bible that included the Apocrypha, and sure enough, there was the book of Judith. What I found in that book was a picture of the last days church, and a big encouragement for those of us hungry for God's glory.

Again, if you're a protestant, please take a deep breath and allow me to explain. First, the books of the Apocrypha are considered by many to be outside the canon of Scripture. Most of them appear to contain historical inac-curacies and questionable sources that might not be extremely important; but, nevertheless, most church leaders do not believe they have the same authority as the canonized Bible. As a result, they have been retained as a sort of appendix to the scriptures.

Even early protestant Bibles still retained the Apocrypha, but that really isn't the point. Whether or not they are God's inspired Word or just "inspirational" on their own merit is not a debate I'm interested in. Personally, I think God could speak through Shakespeare, talking donkeys, or street signs, which would in no way undermine the absolute authority of the Scriptures.

Again, if God needs to tell you something He might choose an unusual way to do it, especially if it gets your attention. And that is exactly what I believe happened to me with the book of Judith. I'm going to summarize the story, using excerpts from the book, and then I want to look at what we can perhaps learn about the last Christians and the Antichrist spirit.

The Book of Judith in Short

Judith was a beautiful woman who lived in the hill country of Israel. She was a widow, and she was well-respected in her community. Here is a quick description of her situation.

> *Judith remained as a widow for three years and four months at home where she set up a tent for herself on the roof of her house. She put sackcloth around her waist and dressed in*

widow's clothing. She fasted all the days of her widowhood, except the day before the Sabbath and the Sabbath itself, the day before the new moon, and the festivals and days of rejoicing of the house of Israel. She was beautiful in appearance, and was very lovely to behold. Her husband Manasseh had left her gold and silver, men and women slaves, livestock, and fields; and she maintained this estate. No one spoke ill of her, for she feared God with great devotion. (Apocrypha, Judith 8:4–8 NRSV)

Later on we learn that she was just as respected for her wisdom as she was for her beauty and holiness; and, as it turned out, she was very courageous, too. While she was living in the hill town of Bethulia, an invading army was setting up camp nearby and planning an attack. The army was sent by King Nebuchadnezzar and was led by a general named Holofernes. The general was greatly feared wherever he went, and he was used to having cities surrender to him even before he got there. This time, however, he was facing Israelites who were in no mood to be taken captive.

All the people in Bethulia humbled themselves and prayed for deliverance as they prepared to defend themselves. When Holofernes saw that they intended to fight he laid siege to the mountain town, intending to wait until they starved to death. He was very sure of himself and his king, Nebuchadnezzar. In fact, he did not think it an injustice to call Nebuchadnezzar a god, and he expected others to do the same. Here is one of his unholy speeches.

What god is there except Nebuchadnezzar? He will send his forces and destroy them from the face of the earth. Their God will not save them; we the king's servants will destroy them as one man. They cannot resist the might of our cavalry. We will overwhelm them; their mountains will be drunk with their blood, and their fields will be full of their dead. Not even their footprints will survive our attack; they will utterly perish. So says King Nebuchadnezzar, lord of the whole earth. For he has spoken; none of his words shall be in vain. (Apocrypha, Judith. 6:2-4 NRSV)

As the siege progressed, the people of Bethulia eventually ran out of water and courage. Their situation was hopeless and they were days away from surrendering their town to Holofernes, when Judith spoke up.

Then Judith said to them, "Listen to me. I am about to do something that will go down through all generations of our descendants. Stand at the town gate tonight so that I may go out with my maid; and within the days after which you have promised to surrender the town to our enemies, the Lord will deliver Israel by my hand. (Apocrypha, Judith 8:32–33 NRSV)

Immediately after those words, Judith cried out to God for help and then prepared herself for the task at hand. She put on all her finest clothes and jewelry and headed out to the enemy's camp. Based on the description of all the fine things she was wearing, she must have been a beautiful sight. The town elders who saw her leave were certainly impressed.

When they saw her transformed in appearance and dressed differently, they were very greatly astounded at her beauty and said to her, "May the God of our ancestors grant you favor and fulfill your plans, so that the people of Israel may glory and Jerusalem may be exalted. She bowed down to God. (Apocrypha, Judith 10:7-8 NRSV)

Judith tricked her way into the enemy camp and right into Holofernes' tent. He was stricken with her, of course, but she kept her distance until an evening when he had drunk himself into a stupor. Holofernes was passed out in his bed when Judith made her move. Above his bed was a canopy that comes into play later.

Holofernes was resting on his bed under a canopy that was woven with purple and gold, emeralds and other precious stones. (Apocrypha, Judith 10:21 NRSV)

As Holofernes lay drunk, Judith offered a prayer and then cut off his head with his own sword. Strangely, when Judith fled the scene, the only things she took with her were the general's head and the canopy over his bed. The next day, when the attackers realized their leader had been beheaded, they ran for their lives and were slaughtered all the way home.

Prepared For Battle

As I mentioned earlier, when I dreamt of the book of Judith, I saw a gold book sitting on a stone table. On the cover was a beautifully adorned bride. Well, Judith is that bride, and when I say "bride" here I am talking metaphorically about the Church, which is called the "wife of the Lamb." However, Judith didn't just look good in a dress; she was courageous, daring, and perfectly equipped to face an evil horde.

In all those ways, she represents the warrior Bride of the last days. She was beautiful, even stunning. Remember the Laodicean church and how the Lord gave them gifts of His glory? All the finery Judith wore into battle was a symbol of that same abundant grace. She was a prophetic picture of a church that had allowed God to shower it with His goodness; but when it came time to fight, she put on His presence like a garment, and His glory was the only the weapon she needed. To God, this would be a beautiful Bride.

If you have never read the book of Judith, but this story sounds somewhat familiar, you might have read about Deborah, Jael, and Sisera in the Old Testament, in Judges, chapter 4. That passage provides another great example of a woman (representing the Bride) overcoming the enemy. But for now, we will stick with Judith in order to see some specific characteristics of the last days church. Judith had been prepared in secret for her eventual battle through her years of fasting and praying. So, when the enemy appeared at the door, she was the only one ready to face him—and all because a foundation of faith had been established in her private devotions.

Now get a picture of a whole group of Christians who, for years, have devoted themselves in secret. They prayed and fasted when no one was watching, specifically so that they would not get any praise from men. They pressed into God's presence until they were intimately familiar with

His goodness. This is the kind of church that can go from humble prayers to courageous warriors in a second. In the last days, fasting is going to be very important. More specifically, living a fasting life will be necessary. Judith fasted and prayed nearly five days of every week; and when you are praying and fasting like that, it is more than a momentary discipline. It is a lifestyle.

However, a fasting lifestyle doesn't necessarily mean abstinence from food. It means a life that is surrendered and is not governed by the needs of the flesh. When fasting is a state of being, it is reflected in every choice we make, as if the need to be close to the Lord supersedes all others. That doesn't mean fasting from food is off the table (pun intended). When we look ahead to the last generation of Enochs, we will see a people so full of God's life that physical food has no hold on them. And it isn't that those Christians will be fasting in order to get something from God; it's that the glory they will experience makes food seem almost unnecessary.

No matter what part of the flesh is being denied, the result is a deeper connection in the Spirit to God's power. And, it is not a coincidence that Judith, a fasting woman who knew how to deny her flesh, was the only one able to confront a very dark adversary. In fact, if you ever feel like you are having a hard time discerning the voice of the Lord, or if you can't seem to break free from the lies of the enemy, start fasting. It doesn't matter if it is one lunch or every meal for 30 days. Nor does it matter if it is food or television. Nothing seems to interrupt the devil's constant barrage of distractions like a good fast.

I am by no means a "superfaster." I have friends who

put me to shame with their discipline in fasting. But I have found that God will use whatever you give Him in faith. So, even if you think you can't do it consistently, like Judith did, just let God lead you in whatever way He thinks is best. The point is not to ignore this very important weapon in our hand. Think of it this way. When the devil is fighting dirty with you (the appliances in your house stop working, the car needs major repair, the kids are sick, and you can't seem to get connected to God...) fasting is the way to "fight dirty" right back.

A Break in the Darkness

The devil Judith faced bears a remarkable resemblance to the one we have been talking about. Holofernes was as anti-Christ as it gets. He openly declared a pagan man to be god and set out to conquer God's people, fitting the evil ruler image perfectly. But, Judith did more than just resist him; she took something very special of his when she defeated him.

Let's take a closer look at the canopy over Holofernes's bed. If you can imagine him looking up at it every night, seeing the jewels twinkle amid a purple background, then you can grasp the desired effect. The canopy was made to look like the heavens, and the symbolism shouldn't be lost on us.

The air around us is an unseen battleground between holy and fallen angels. Some of these fallen angels occupy a space in the heavens where they inject their lies and wicked influence. We can see the evidence of their influence in areas where a certain problem is prevalent. It might be a certain kind of crime, or even a specific mental state.

For instance, have you ever driven into an unfamiliar town and just felt icky? Or, have you ever visited a place and seen so much of a certain condition, like alcoholism, that you couldn't write it off as merely coincidental? On the other extreme, have you ever been in a place that had far too many churches of far too many varieties—and it left you feeling a little too "religious"?

All these are clues as to what is in the air above that country, or town, or family. It has all been passed off as nothing more sinister than human nature, but it could just as easily be the influence of a fallen angel. Because if the good angels are there to help us, then the bad ones are equally bent on hurting us. Listen to the advice the Apostle Paul gives concerning these wicked spirits:

> *Put on the full armor of God, so that you will be able to stand firm against the schemes of the devil. For our struggle is not against flesh and blood, but against the rulers, against the powers, against the world forces of this darkness, against the spiritual forces of wickedness in the heavenly places. (Ephesians 6:11-13 NASU)*

The spiritual forces of evil, including the Antichrist spirit, work and live in the heavenly places. Some have taken up residence and spent centuries oozing their specific perversions over whole groups of people. However, Paul said it is still our struggle, which means that those evil beings should not get to sit up there uncontested. Everything has been put under Jesus' feet, and that includes every angel, fallen or not. So, when someone comes along and opposes those wicked powers by invoking the authority of Jesus, those devils have more than met their match.

When Judith cut off Holofernes's head and took down his canopy, she was a symbol of the warrior Bride expelling the Antichrist spirit and removing his place in the heavens. Think of the canopy as a heavenly covering or area of influence. In our modern vernacular, we have a military term called a "no-fly zone." It's a stretch of airspace that is off limits to all aircraft other than military or government planes. Think of Judith's victory as a symbolic "no-fly zone." The warrior Bride took over the Antichrist's airspace, and now a whole area previously under darkness could experience the glory. She took away his influence in the heavens.

In the last days, there will be Christians empowered by God's glory, and the air above them will be a no-Antichrist zone. It won't matter if they are persecuted even to death; their intimacy with Jesus will be the foil to the Antichrist's lies. They will also represent the last chance humanity has to hear the good news. When they enter a place, the lies of the Antichrist and the authority of his government will be pushed back, and the hearers will be able to listen without that wicked influence. For that moment, the glory of God will be the only influence, and the people will have the opportunity to enter into God's Kingdom before it's too late.

You can apply this to your own life right now. If you take the time to deal with the lies you have believed, then you will experience a no-Antichrist zone, too. Then, when people come to you in need, they will find a glory zone where the only things allowed to fly in the air above you are holy angels and the Spirit of God.

The opposition is tough and the lies are subtle and ubiquitous, but that doesn't mean we are without hope. Remember that no matter how much you have suffered because of the devil's schemes, the Lord will always use all of that to bring you into the riches of His glory. And even though the spiritual climate in our world is about to change, God has given us an invitation to His communion table. Once there, we will remain untouched by the coming apostasy. Our strategy in this battle should never change. Keep getting closer to Jesus and let His glory saturate you.

7

IN THE SPIRIT

Just before Jesus was crucified He shared a meal with His disciples, which we typically call the Last Supper. It was a moment of intense fulfillment because the meal was a celebration of the Hebrew Passover, and Jesus was about to be the Passover sacrifice. Also, at this moment, some important things finally clicked into place for the Apostles.

It was an especially important moment for the Apostle John, and it seems fitting that the Lord would ask him to write the longest account of that intimate meeting. He was sitting right next to Jesus, and the Scriptures give us a beautiful picture of the relationship they must have shared. We find it right as Jesus prophesies His betrayal:

> *When Jesus had said this, He became troubled in spirit, and testified and said, "Truly, truly, I say to you, that one of you will betray Me." The disciples began looking at one another, at a loss to know of which one He was speaking. There was reclining on Jesus' bosom one of His disciples, whom Jesus loved. So Simon Peter gestured to him, and said to him, "Tell us who it is of whom He is speaking." He, leaning back thus on Jesus' bosom, said to Him, "Lord, who is it?" (John 13:21–26 NASU)*

You really have to put yourself in John's shoes for this to sink in. Imagine yourself at the Passover meal, leaning up against Jesus. The above passage says John was reclining on Jesus' bosom, so put yourself in that position in your mind. Can you imagine laying on the Son of God, with your head resting on His chest? If you have ever rested your head on someone like that, then you know how easy it is to hear their heartbeat. John had been listening to the steady rhythm of Jesus' heart the entire meeting. Through Jesus' bosom he was hearing the heartbeat of God.

I don't think it is coincidence that when Jesus mentioned someone betraying Him, Peter looked at John for the explanation. They all knew he was close to Jesus, and his posture at the table reflected his adoration for Jesus in everything. It might seem like John was as close to Jesus as was humanly possible, but that is not the end of the story.

The Advantage of the Spirit

Just moments after we read about John reclining on the Lord, Jesus makes an arresting statement.

> *"But I tell you the truth, it is to your advantage that I go away; for if I do not go away, the Helper will not come to you; but if I go, I will send Him to you. (John 16:7–8)*

When I imagine myself listening to Jesus' heartbeat, it's easy to think, "It can't get any better than this." It just seems so intimate and personal; it would be hard to beat an experience like that. But then, Jesus has the audacity to say, "I know that you are all enjoying My Presence here, but it would be better for you if I left" (my paraphrase, of course).

If I were John I might have said, "No, wait! Don't leave! This is the closest I have ever been to God; You can't leave now!" That would have been a reasonable response. However, I don't think Jesus told them in a random way, at an arbitrary moment, that He was on His way out. He waited until they were all together in the most intimate setting before He told them there was something even better in store. In other words, the Last Supper was the closest they had ever been with Jesus, and that was especially true for John. Nevertheless, Jesus told them that there would soon be an even greater intimacy with the Lord to be experienced, and it was going to come through the "Helper," the Holy Spirit.

God never moves His people backwards. From the book of Genesis all the way through the Bible to the book of Revelation, there is never a point in the history of man's relationship with God in which the story stalled and regressed. Even while Israel was constantly falling in and out of God's favor, the story was still moving forward. So, here in the gospel of John, right when it seems someone has reached the absolute pinnacle in their relationship with the Lord, we see that God still has more He wants us to experience. Apparently, walking around the earth with Jesus does not represent the best it can get.

So, ask yourself this question: If you could have Jesus right next to you, and you were allowed to rest your head on His bosom for as long as you liked, would you take that over your present relationship with God? If any of us answer "yes" to that question, it could be a sure sign that we have missed at least some of the blessing of the Holy Spirit.

To me, John's moment with Jesus is a picture of a near-perfect relationship with the Lord, and that should tell us "by default" just how big a deal the Holy Spirit is. If knowing Jesus through the Spirit is better than that, then it must be really, really good! So good, in fact, that we can experience more of Jesus through the Spirit than we could even if He were sitting right next to us.

The Spirit in Revelation

Back when I was in college, I remember reading the book of Revelation and noticing a curious omission. I kept reading about God sitting on the throne, and there were ample mentions of the Lamb of God, but where was the third part of the Holy Trinity? We know God has expressed Himself as Father, Son, and Holy Spirit; but I was only seeing the first two when I read Revelation.

I can remember thinking, "Lord, if John saw the Father on the throne and then a Lamb sitting there as well, was it too much trouble for him to see a big white dove, too?" We have plenty of familiar images for the Holy Spirit, a white dove being fairly standard, so in my opinion it would have made more sense for all of them to be there. Again, even at the end of Revelation when we read a description of the New Heavens and the New Earth, we still only get two out of three.

> *Then he showed me a river of the water of life, clear as crystal, coming from the throne of God and of the Lamb, in the middle of its street. On either side of the river was the tree of life, bearing twelve kinds of fruit, yielding its fruit every month; and the leaves of the tree were for the healing of the nations. There will no longer be any curse; and the throne of God and of the Lamb will be in it. (Revelations 22:1–3)*

For years I wondered where the Holy Spirit was in all of this, and why He doesn't get to sit on the throne with the other two parts of the Godhead. I only started to understand when God prompted the question, "Where was John when he saw the visions written in Revelation?" My immediate answer was, "On the island of Patmos, of course," but then I realized again that God rarely asks questions you already know the answer to. A closer look at the scriptures then revealed where John really was that day.

> *I, John, your brother and fellow partaker in the tribulation and kingdom and perseverance which are in Jesus, was on the island called Patmos because of the word of God and the testimony of Jesus. I was in the Spirit on the Lord's day, and I heard behind me a loud voice like the sound of a trumpet... (Revelations 1:9-11)*

His body might have been on Patmos, but John, himself, was in the Spirit. That was the actual location of his persona, which explains a lot about the book of Revelation and the Holy Spirit. John didn't see a white dove when he looked at the throne because he was in the Spirit, so he saw everything from within that part of the Godhead. It would be the same as if you were inside person A, looking out at persons B and C. You would say, "I see persons B and C." It's not that person A isn't there; you are just inside of him. And that brings us back to something from a previous chapter. When God sent the Holy Spirit, the invitation was to come experience Him from within a part of Himself. At that moment, the relationship became internal instead of external.

You can see why marriage is used in the Bible to describe the relationship between Jesus and the Church. In marriage, a man and woman come together as one flesh. In a sense, they know each other internally, and that concept is played out far more deeply with the advent of the Holy Spirit. It is God's invitation to know Him from within, with no outside barriers. Now we can start to see why Jesus told his disciples that it was better if He left, because there was a deeper relationship yet to be discovered. Furthermore, since Jesus is not walking around the earth in physical form, knowing Him through the Spirit is the only way possible. So, not only is it better, it really is the only option. We can tie that right back to our discussion of the lies so many people hear in their heads.

If there is an Antichrist spirit roaming around injecting a version of Jesus into our minds that is tainted with lies, then the only way to recognize the true Jesus is through the Holy Spirit. But if the world is full of Christians disconnected from God's Spirit, how will they know the difference?

The book of Revelation had other titles throughout history. It has been called "The Apocalypse of John," or "The

Revelation of John." One of my favorite alternate names is "The Revealing of Jesus Christ." I think that is an appropriate title because that's what the book really does. It pulls back the veil and shows us Jesus for who He really is, and there is no other way to see Him like that except from within the Holy Spirit.

Holy Spirit Immersion

As I mentioned before, I experienced the Holy Spirit for the first time in college. During that revival, I began questioning a lot of what I had been taught while I was growing up in church. I became particularly interested in what the Bible called the baptism of the Holy Spirit. I was seeing the work of the Spirit all around me, and I could hear God's voice clearer than ever, but I couldn't shake this thought that I had never been baptized in the Holy Spirit. I had been baptized in water when I was eleven, but I knew there was something more. Here is what John the Baptist had to say about how Jesus baptizes.

> *John answered and said to them all, "As for me, I baptize you with water; but One is coming who is mightier than I, and I am not fit to untie the thong of His sandals; He will baptize you with the Holy Spirit and fire. (Luke 3:16–17)*

I kept asking people about it in the hope that someone could explain it to me, or could just pray for me to have it. Eventually, a wonderful Spirit-filled woman saw my need and offered to pray for me.

The results were immediate. As soon as she prayed for me I saw a vision, and I lost the feeling in my hands and mouth. In the vision, I was sitting on a pew in a church, and large metal chains were wrapped around my arms and fastened to the pew. I knew the interpretation even as I saw it. I was chained to my old understanding of how church and my relationship with God should be, and now the Lord was breaking me free. From that moment on, I felt a release to experience the Holy Spirit; but I can remember struggling with the concept quite a bit before I finally yielded. Since I was raised in traditional protestant churches, the baptism of the Holy Spirit carried strong doctrinal implications and was generally off limits.

Part of the problem in receiving the full blessing of the Spirit is man's pride. People have a hard time letting go and submitting to the Lord. They are afraid of what God might tell them to do, or maybe they are afraid of losing their dignity. Another problem that is just as hard to overcome is the misunderstanding of what baptism really is. Baptism means immersion. It is the act of completely inundating yourself in something—in this case, the Holy Spirit. Over time, Christians have taken that concept and intellectualized it into a doctrine. Once it is in our heads as a doctrine, we feel the right to choose it or reject it according to our denominational preference, but it is the meaning of the words that is important.

If God were giving you the opportunity to immerse yourself in a part of His divine Trinity, then wouldn't you jump in with both feet?

Instead of spending our time deciding if it makes us a Pentecostal or not, let's just receive the blessing. The free gift of the Holy Spirit is a wondrous gesture on God's part, reflecting His desire to be one with His children. We would be crazy not to receive it. Listen to how the Apostle Paul speaks of baptism:

> *There is one body and one Spirit, just as also you were called in one hope of your calling; one Lord, one faith, one baptism, one God and Father of all who is over all and through all and in all. (Ephesians 4:4–6 NASU)*

We read before that Jesus came to baptize us with the Holy Spirit and with fire, so which baptism do you think Paul is referring to as the "one" baptism? Water baptism is important, don't get me wrong; but it is only a symbol of what has taken place in the heart of the believer. If you had to choose which was more critical, would you take the symbol or the real thing that Jesus came to give us?

Not that we have to choose; both are important and prescribed, and there are times in the Bible when they happen both simultaneously and separately. And despite all the doctrines that try to explain or categorize how and when it is supposed to happen, I still think the major issue is what God is telling us through the words, themselves.

So when we talk about immersion, we are talking about getting your whole person into the living water of the Spirit. Some people might have a toe in and others might be wading up to their waists—but a true baptism means you go under all the way.

Made in His Image

We were made to experience God in the Spirit. As awkward or unnatural as it can sometimes feel, God created us with the specific capacity to know Him that way; it was engineered into us from the very beginning.

> *Then God said, "Let Us make man in Our image, according to Our likeness..." (Genesis 1:26)*

That statement is packed with metaphysical meaning, so let's take a quick look at how it plays out. Many scholars, Christian or not, agree that a human is made up of three individual but specific parts. We have a body, a soul, and a spirit. We have a good handle on what our body is, but our soul and our spirit can be a little harder to discern. Our soul houses our intellect, will, and emotions; and our spirit is that part of us that is simply spiritual. You can think of it like this: Your intellect, will, and emotions (your soul) determine who you are and what you do. Your body is the physical vessel for your soul and spirit, which allows you to interact with the material world. And your spirit is the part of you that connects and interacts with everything in the unseen dimension.

Furthermore, the three main parts of ourselves (i.e., body, soul, and spirit) are perfect copies of the Lord's metaphysical makeup as well. God has revealed Himself as Father,

Son, and Holy Spirit. The Holy Spirit is... well, the Spirit. The Father is the intellect, will, and emotions of the Godhead. And, the Son is the physical representation of the Lord. Look at these scriptures that describe Jesus' nature and how the "will" of the Godhead is attributed to the Father:

> *He is the image of the invisible God, the firstborn of all creation. (Colossians 1:15–16)*

> *For in Him all the fullness of Deity dwells in bodily form. (Colossians 2:9)*

> *Truly, truly, I say to you, the Son can do nothing of Himself, unless it is something He sees the Father doing; for whatever the Father does, these things the Son also does in like manner. (John 5:19-20)*

> *For I have come down from heaven, not to do My own will, but the will of Him who sent Me. (John 6:38)*

God's physical representation is Jesus. He is the outward expression that also houses God's two invisible parts. But before we go deeper into that, let's revisit a concept from earlier in this chapter—the Trinity. Everyone has a hard time grasping that idea, but seeing how you have been made in God's image can shed some light on it. Even though you are made up of three different parts, you don't ever feel like three different people are living inside you. So, as hard as it is to understand how God is three elements in one, we are just the same and it seems to work all right for us.

God's three parts are perfectly unified, which is why Genesis 1:26 uses both the singular noun, God, and the plural pronouns Us and Our. He is three parts, but one person; and we have been made like Him, right down to our metaphysical structure.

> *Then God said, "Let Us make man in Our image, according to Our likeness; (Genesis 1:26)*

The Unseen Realm

Going back to the verses about Jesus, take note that He is called the image or bodily form of God. The other two aspects of God's persona are invisible in the physical realm. Likewise, when we examine ourselves, we realize that two of our own parts are also invisible in the physical realm. However, since the majority of our persona is unseen, even though we're not usually as aware of it, the invisible realm might therefore be a very important aspect of life—of ourselves. We can see in the physical realm easily enough with our natural eyes, and we know how to move and live in that dimension; but it is equally (if not more) important to perceive and to "live in" the other dimension as well.

More than that, God made you (and specifically equipped you!) to exist in the spiritual realm as naturally as you do in the physical one—which is one of the things that makes humanity so special. Indeed, when we let God transform us back into what He created us to be, we start to see things far outside the boundaries of our physical, material lives.

To get some scriptural context, read what Paul said to the Ephesians and Corinthians:

> *I pray that the eyes of your heart may be enlightened, so that you will know what is the hope of His calling, what are the riches of the glory of His inheritance in the saints, and what is the surpassing greatness of His power toward us who believe. (Ephesians 1:18–19)*

When Paul prays for the "eyes" of their hearts, he is not being poetic or using a figure of speech. We have a whole other set of eyes from which we can perceive reality—we just need them to be enlightened.

> *For momentary, light affliction is producing for us an eternal weight of glory far beyond all comparison, while we look not at the things which are seen, but at the things which are not seen; for the things which are seen are temporal, but the things which are not seen are eternal. (2 Corinthians 4:17–18)*

Here, the church is instructed to look at the things that are unseen. Well, how do you see invisible things? You have to reconnect with the part of you that was made to perceive what is invisible to the natural eye. Remember, you were created to exist in both realms; that is part of being made in God's image. By the way, as mentioned in the previous chapter, the above is why fasting is so important. When you fast, you force yourself to focus on the spiritual realm. You are denying your flesh, and the only place to go is into the Spirit.

But, there is no denying that it can be difficult. In this present world, the devil has done a great deal to make sure that none of us focus on the unseen realm, which makes perfect sense given that he lives there. The wicked spiritual powers know that when Christians allow themselves to be immersed in the Spirit, they can perceive every evil strategy being implemented. Even better, they can see God's plans, too!

The devil has spent thousands of years convincing humanity to deny the spiritual realm (or to misunderstand it), and this is especially true in our western, developed civilization. Is it any wonder then that, with all our knowledge and technology, we have convinced ourselves that we are too smart for anything unseen? Modern man has ignored an aspect of life just as real as the material world, and it is serving the devil's purposes perfectly.

However, when Christians immerse themselves in God's Holy Spirit, that frustrates his plan over and over again. That baptism awakens our senses and puts us back in contact with the spiritual realm. Then, as we yield to His Spirit, we realize that what was previously invisible is now very, very real.

A Quick Summary

Before we move on, I want to insert a quick summary of what we have discussed. First, being immersed in the Holy Spirit is a crucial part of Christianity. It isn't an option or doctrinal preference; it is God's plan for every believer. Living in the Spirit is what allows us to see Jesus for who He is, and it connects us with His love and His blessings in ways that surpass knowledge.

Second, and this goes back to some previous chapters, receiving God's goodness is all about learning to believe Him. Remember, if you are receiving His glory, then you know Him as He is. You have a singular understanding of His goodness; and being with Him means being in the safest, most loving place you could be. In other words, receiving God's goodness and being immersed in His Spirit both work together to bring you to a place of intimacy with the Lord. God's deepest desire is to know and be known by His children, and everything in history is meant to point to that. It is about knowing Him. Period.

Once you know that, there is nothing to keep you out of His presence. You realize that Jesus has done everything for you. He has forgiven you, filled you with His Spirit, and brought you before the Father—and it had nothing to do with you. Your effort had nothing to do with His blessings. You can have the privilege of walking in heavenly places, but not because you're so good you deserve it. It's all because Jesus made a way for you. That understanding is what opens the door and gets you into the flow of His Spirit, so you can live life unbound by material restraints. Even more, it's what allows us to affect this present world with Heaven's power.

Walking in Heaven

At the beginning of Revelation, it says John was "in the Spirit on the Lord's day." That is a state of being we can all be in as often as we want if we yield ourselves to Him. In that position, God can take you anywhere He wants, and He can show you in so many creative ways how much He loves you

The first time I knew I was in the Spirit, I found myself standing before God's throne. In some ways it was like seeing a vision, only it lasted a long time and I felt like a part of me was actually *physically* there. The throne was huge and made of something like white marble. There were steps leading up to the throne, as I took a step up, I could feel His love and acceptance—and with each step it got stronger and stronger.

I arrived at the top and could feel the presence of the Father. He looked full of energy, as if the different aspects of creation were swirling around His seated figure. He motioned with His hand to the side, and I could see a door opening up to the most pristine, lush garden. Then I could hear the invitation spoken into my mind, "You can come here and talk with Me as often as you like."

I have since gone back to that garden, and other places in Heaven, whenever I've had the chance. And every time I go, I encounter something new and different. The Spirit takes me on a journey, and sometimes I am confronted by the areas of my life that need to change. At other times, He just lets me see things to get to know Him better. No matter what happens, I am always left in awe of His love for me.

When I walked into that garden with the Lord for the first time, I was instantly struck by how much life I could feel there. It felt like all the trees and the grasses were alive because He was alive. It all responded to His abundant life. I saw other people there, and everyone was naked, although not in the sense we would normally think. They were gloriously naked, and the environment was one hundred percent shame-free.

I walked over to a man seated by a gold easel, and I was curious about what He was designing on the paper. I could see a little of what he was drawing, but I kept feeling an urge to look at the man, himself. When I finally focused on his face, I discovered it was me. God was showing me my life in the New Heavens and Earth. I marveled at how unhurried this version of me was, and how much he/I was enjoying every little detail.

On another occasion, I went to a classroom in the garden. When I sat down, a book opened in front of me and I could read the entire parable of the mustard seed in the gospel of Matthew. Later that day, I made sure to look at my physical Bible to make sure what I saw was correct. It was, word for word.

> *He presented another parable to them, saying, "The kingdom of heaven is like a mustard seed, which a man took and sowed in his field; and this is smaller than all other seeds, but when it is full grown, it is larger than the garden plants and becomes a tree, so that the birds of the air come and nest in its branches." (Matthew 13:31–32)*

To be honest, up until that point I hadn't thought much about that parable. I figured it was God's way of saying that His kingdom is really big, even though it started from humble beginnings. But the Lord explained it to me a little differently as I sat reading it in Heaven.

A Powerful Expression of Faith

If you will start to experience Heaven through the Spirit, even if it is just the smallest portion of your day or week, it will grow into a powerful expression of your faith. And the more familiar with Heaven you become, the more it starts to occupy the space all around you and affect the natural world. As Heaven's influence grows, so does the amount of angelic involvement in your life. They are "the birds of the air" that will come to rest with anyone willing to step into the unseen realm.

There is also a big encouragement for us in that experience. If we are ever persecuted and our Bibles are taken from us, you can read as much as you want in the Spirit. Everything is available for us in Heaven; and when we walk in the Spirit, we can access all of it. So of course there is a Bible in Heaven that we can read. It's God's Word after all.

To give an example of how all this affects the natural realm, I remember an experience in the Spirit in which I found myself walking with Jesus in a portico fronting a garden. I can remember feeling anxious because it just felt too easy to be walking with Jesus in the spiritual realm. Remember, it does feel a little unnatural at first. I kept thinking, "You just can't walk with Jesus in Heaven—that's not supposed to be possible!"

Almost instantly, I felt the Lord calm me down and say, "Take whatever time you need to get comfortable." It took me about ten minutes before I could go on; but when I did, we just started walking down that covered path. As we walked, I could feel Him drawing me close to Him and I asked Him, "Are we going anywhere today?"

He told me He just wanted to walk and talk with me for a while. I talked with Him about all sorts of things and sometimes felt the need to make requests. I would start with, "I pray that... " but He would stop me and tell me to talk to Him like I would anyone else. So, instead, I would say, "I really need your help with... "

I asked Him that day for help with one of our children, who was going through a tough time; and as soon as I did, an angel came up beside us. Jesus whispered to the angel and he immediately flew away again. I asked the Lord who the angel was and I heard the scripture verse:

> *Their (the children's) angels in heaven continually see the face of My Father who is in heaven. (Matthew 18:10)*

I was amazed that as soon as I asked for help for one of my kids, the Lord called my child's angel in, gave him instructions, and then sent him back to help. It should come as no surprise that we saw an immediate difference, which shows us part of the blessing of walking in the Spirit. When we are in the Spirit with Him, what happens in the unseen realm affects the physical one.

Every journey in the Spirit has made me fall in love with the Lord more and more, and that's why the invitation is there in the first place. As I have said before, I am sure being in the Spirit is different for everyone, but the end result is the same. The whole experience draws us deeper into God and leaves us wanting more of Him than anything else in this world.

This kind of interaction with Heaven isn't a new thing. The early church had a great understanding of an unseen heavenly realm where they could interact with God in the Spirit. We already saw it in John's recording of Revelation, but here it is again in the book of Ephesians.

> *Blessed be the God and Father of our Lord Jesus Christ, who has blessed us with every spiritual blessing in the heavenly places in Christ. (Ephesians 1:3)*

We have to ask ourselves, would God give us every spiritual blessing and then put them in a place where we can't access them? Absolutely not. He made us to experience life in the Spirit so that we could receive all the blessings of Jesus. However, our reluctance to live beyond the world we can see has limited our understanding of Him; it has blocked out a whole dynamic way that God reveals His love. Yet when we let go and trust the Holy Spirit, He will reveal to us the love of Jesus in ways that we have never imagined.

Again, that's what walking in the Spirit is all about; getting in contact with the all-surpassing love of God. When you walk in the heavenly places in the Spirit, from there you will see things, hear things, and feel things that go beyond any natural understanding. This is part of the greater intimacy that Jesus promised at the Lord's Supper. He knew it was to our advantage that He was leaving in a physical sense, because the Holy Spirit was going to open up an entirely new dimension in man's relationship with God.

The experiences I just mentioned are only scratching the surface of what's possible, and I can't wait to see what God has in store for me tomorrow and the day after that. God made us to experience life like this. We are supposed to be a people who bridge the gap between Heaven and earth, and it is all possible because of God's totally free gift—the Holy Spirit. We just need to let go and allow Him to take us on a journey. Better yet, let's dive in head first and get immersed.

8

A PROPHETIC PICTURE

In the end times there won't be a convenient middle ground. A generation of believers walking in God's glory, and an Antichrist government, will emerge in parallel paths and everyone will have to choose one or the other. Anyone who thinks he can be neutral will, in fact, have chosen the Antichrist. And everyone whose heart is turned to the Lord will find himself accelerated into a glorious communion.

Christians who are hungry for God's glory are the forerunners of the last Christian generation; which means our job is to live like they will—*right now.* In doing so, we are paving the road for all other believers who will live in a time when God's glory is a matter of spiritual survival. Even if you don't think you will ever see those days, it doesn't exclude you from living the same glory-filled life. In fact, the more Christians experience God's abundant glory now, the more the power of the Antichrist will start to emerge as well. The two are completely related. One won't increase unless the other increases—because they are locked together in an end-times fulfillment.

In other words, once you decide to pursue a life of intimacy with God, you become a last days believer. The more Christians all over the world start to experience that kind of intimacy, the more the Antichrist government will arise until the final stage, set with a glorious, warrior Bride overcoming the Antichrist's reign. Believers walking in an unhindered connection to Heaven will be the proof that we are in the final days.

Stephen, the First Martyr

To get a sense of what Christianity will be like in the last days, we need to look at the story of Stephen the martyr. He is a prototype for believers who are experiencing God's glory, yet are facing intense persecution. In case you are unfamiliar with his life and ministry, here is a brief summation: Stephen was a Christian in Jerusalem during the very beginnings of the faith, and he was called upon to serve at a time when the Apostles needed help meeting the needs of a growing church. The Apostles asked for wise men of good reputation and full of the Spirit–and in Stephen they got what they asked for.

> *Stephen, full of grace and power, was performing great wonders and signs among the people. But some men from what was called the Synagogue of the Freedmen, including both Cyrenians and Alexandrians, and some from Cilicia and Asia, rose up and argued with Stephen. But they were unable to cope with the wisdom and the Spirit with which he was speaking. (Acts 6:8–11 NASU)*

As you can guess, his opponents weren't about to let

him keep preaching, so they trumped up some charges of blasphemy and took him to court. After a slew of people gave falsified testimonies, Stephen was allowed to speak. When he did, he gave one of the most profound and convicting sermons ever recorded (far too much material to be discussed here). And it was those inspired words that finally got him killed.

However, before he began speaking, the crowd noticed something peculiar about Stephen's appearance:

> *And fixing their gaze on him, all who were sitting in the Council saw his face like the face of an angel. (Acts 6:15)*

If I said that someone's face looked like an angel, what's the first thing that would pop into your head? Most people imagine him glowing, and that would seem accurate because it was enough of a display to make the crowd fix their gaze on him. And it wasn't just a peaceful looking face, because that wouldn't have prompted the whole crowd to take notice. Neither would it have been mentioned in the Scriptures. It must have been something strange enough to make "all who were sitting in the Council" pause, so a glow or a radiance is probably the most likely explanation.

No one in the Bible who saw an angel ever said they looked peaceful. In fact, their arrival was often accompanied by the words, "Do not be afraid." That should tell us that our modern chubby baby or fairy like image of angels is way off the mark. If a normal human response to an angel is fear, then they must be intimidating at the very least. A face like an angel would therefore be a sight to behold. This is what happened next, after Stephen gave his speech.

> *Now when they heard this they were cut to the quick, and they*
> *began gnashing their teeth at him. But being full of the Holy*
> *Spirit, he gazed intently into heaven and saw the glory of God,*
> *and Jesus standing at the right hand of God; and he said,*
> *"Behold, I see the heavens opened up and the Son of Man*
> *standing at the right hand of God." But they cried out with a*
> *loud voice, and covered their ears and rushed at him with one*
> *impulse. When they had driven him out of the city, they began*
> *stoning him; and the witnesses laid aside their robes at the feet*
> *of a young man named Saul. They went on stoning Stephen as*
> *he called on the Lord and said, "Lord Jesus, receive my spirit!"*
> *Then falling on his knees, he cried out with a loud voice, "Lord,*
> *do not hold this sin against them!" Having said this, he fell*
> *asleep. (Acts 7:54–60)*

Dying in the Glory

During Stephen's last moments, it seems as if he was totally
unaffected by the violence—and his was an extremely violent
death. Even as the crowd is pummeling him with rocks, he
manages to call on the Lord and forgive his oppressors. After
that, he simply fell asleep.

Stephen wasn't a powerless prisoner being led off to
his death; rather, he demonstrated an abnormal amount of
control over the whole situation. He gave up his spirit and
fell asleep only after he said what he needed to, so he wasn't

necessarily at the mercy of the rocks.

The truth is, the only part of Stephen being hit by rocks was his body. His spirit had been communing with the Lord from the moment they dragged him to court, as evidenced by his angelic face. Stephen was able to show remarkable poise because he was in the Spirit at that very moment. To him, a part of his persona was in the physical realm suffering violence, but the other part of him was in the glory of God.

As stated earlier, in the last days, communing with God in the Spirit will be a matter of spiritual survival. At that time, the persecution will be as intense as it has ever been before, if not worse. However, the devil's reason for persecuting Christians is rarely to kill them; it's to make them give up on or renounce their faith. This is why persecution is seldom carried out in a systematic or clinical way. It is always violent, as if the oppressors are looking for more and more horrific ways to kill and maim God's chosen. Just a quick look at the history of Christian martyrs shows the lengths to which the devil will go to try to scare people out of their faith.

What will make that strategy worthless will be a whole generation of believers who know their bodies are not the source of their lives. They will know how to relate to God in the Spirit, and they will live as naturally in that realm as they do in the physical one. It doesn't matter what will happen to them in the body because they will be walking in Heaven everyday. That last generation of Enochs will be unpersecutable.

Walking in God's glory not only makes for a peaceful death, it also allows the believer to do something totally unexpected—to forgive. Stephen gives his killers the exact same blessing as Jesus gave His when He was crucified. They both pray that God will forgive their oppressors, and that is the testimony of someone who is saturated with God's love. So, if there is one hallmark of the last Christians, it will be the ability to forgive in the midst of unprecedented persecution. Only a deep connection to Heaven would allow a person to do something so un-human, and it is another example of how the last generation of Enochs will release God's glory.

A few chapters back, we saw how releasing God's goodness doesn't always sound good. Sometimes it is a powerful rebuke or portent of judgment. But we also saw God's desire to couple those strong words with a demonstration of His goodness. Stephen played this out perfectly. He gave a scathing sermon that made his hearers gnash their teeth and cover their ears. But then, at his death, he performed a miracle. He gave them the gift of undeserved forgiveness. To really understand the significance of that, we need to look at a biblical principle that is every bit as miraculous as healing the blind or parting the seas.

The Miracle of Forgiveness

Jesus was known for drawing a crowd, and sometimes the people were packed so tightly, someone determined to get to him had to go through the roof. When four friends of a paralytic were confronted by the masses, that is exactly what they did to get their friend some help. However, when they finally got him there, Jesus did not immediately respond as expected.

> *And they came, bringing to Him a paralytic, carried by four men. Being unable to get to Him because of the crowd, they removed the roof above Him; and when they had dug an opening, they let down the pallet on which the paralytic was lying. And Jesus seeing their faith said to the paralytic, "Son, your sins are forgiven." But some of the scribes were sitting there and reasoning in their hearts, "Why does this man speak that way? He is blaspheming; who can forgive sins but God alone?" Immediately Jesus, aware in His spirit that they were reasoning that way within themselves, said to them, "Why are you reasoning about these things in your hearts? "Which is easier, to say to the paralytic, 'Your sins are forgiven'; or to say, 'Get up, and pick up your pallet and walk'? "But so that you may know that the Son of Man has authority on earth to forgive sins" —He said to the paralytic, "I say to you, get up, pick up your pallet and go home." (Mark 2:3–11)*

Jesus has a knack for doing the unexpected; and in this situation, He really stunned the crowd. Everyone thought He would see the desperation of the paralytic and heal him, but they did not expect Him to forgive his sins. However, Jesus was doing a greater miracle in forgiving him. Hence His words: "Which is easier... your sins are forgiven, or... get up and walk." To understand what a big deal forgiveness is, let's look at a passage from Isaiah.

> *"I, even I, am the one who wipes out your transgressions for My own sake, And I will not remember your sins. (Is. 43:25)*

How does an omniscient God, who knows everything all the time, not remember something? This is why forgiveness is such a miracle; God is wiping something from His divine memory forever. Even the paralysis the man was suffering from was a temporary problem with a temporary solution. He was only paralyzed on this earth for this comparably short life, yet the forgiveness he received lasts for eternity.

When God forgives, He alters His own recollection of history, which doesn't mean He can't remember the moment you lied—He just remembers it differently. Instead of seeing you make the wrong choice, He sees you in the light of Jesus' forgiveness, and He decides on His own to remember you perfect, rather than remember you steeped in your flaws.

Therefore, when Jesus forgave the man, He changed the heavenly record all the way back to the man's birth—and forever changed the divine mind of God. Afterward, when He healed the man of his condition, He altered the shape and function of his spinal cord and backbone. The shift that took place in the cosmos when Jesus forgave him was far greater than the one that restored the man's body.

Also, Jesus is making a point here about how a person receives forgiveness. In the passage about the paralytic, Jesus discerns the minds of two separate groups. He notices the faith of the man's friends, versus the doubting thoughts of the crowd. Interestingly, there is not one mention of what the paralyzed man was thinking. The scriptures can say just as much by what they omit as by what they include. So if everyone in this scene is getting their mind read but the man, then there must be a good reason for that. I think Jesus was showing everyone that forgiveness had nothing to do with them.

The paralytic didn't utter one word during the entire event. He never said, "Lord, I believe!" He didn't call Jesus "Messiah" or "Rabbi" either. He never even got to ask for anything. Jesus could have discerned his thoughts like He did everyone else in the room, but to Him it didn't matter if the man even believed in Him or not. He gave him forgiveness as a gift.

Jesus has done the same thing for all of us. He has already forgiven us of everything we will ever do wrong, and it has nothing to do with us—certainly not with our worth. If it did, then *we* would be responsible for gaining God's forgiveness, which would lead us to be legalistic and self-righteous. You can't earn God's pardon; you just have to receive the miracle.

Giving Forgiveness

The Church today is hungry for God to demonstrate His power to heal. We all know it's possible, and every year we become more comfortable believing God for it. However, we tend to be much less aggressive in giving out the miracle of forgiveness ourselves. Everyone knows how hard it is to forgive someone who hurt us when they show no interest of owning up to their faults. The truth is, they need forgiveness (and we need to let it go, too), but we struggle with giving it out freely. Deep down, we need them to say they're sorry before we forgive them; but if the same person were dying of cancer, we would be praying for them without any thoughts about their worthiness.

Then there are the people who haven't done anything wrong to you, or maybe you don't even know them. Yet they need forgiveness too, and it just might be our job to extend that miracle to them. Look at what Jesus said to His disciples after He rose from the grave:

> *He breathed on them and said to them, "Receive the Holy Spirit. If you forgive the sins of any, their sins have been forgiven them; if you retain the sins of any, they have been retained." (John 20:22–23)*

This is quite a responsibility, but try to think of healing, miracles, and forgiveness as the same kind of supernatural outpouring. If God could use us to do the first two, couldn't He use us for the last one? This is where we might have a hesitation because of our doctrine. We have believed for a long time that forgiveness is the same as salvation; yet although they are connected, they are not the same thing. To see the difference, read some of Jesus' last words while hanging on the cross.

> *When they came to the place called The Skull, there they crucified Him and the criminals, one on the right and the other on the left. But Jesus was saying, "Father, forgive them; for they do not know what they are doing." (Luke 23:33–34)*

Was everyone within earshot forgiven? Yes. The Lord only did what He saw the Father in Heaven doing. So if He forgave the people crucifying Him, it was because the Father was doing the same thing. Did that mean everyone Jesus forgave while hanging on the cross was saved and born again? No.

Being born again is what happens when a person receives all that God has done for them. It is the moment when someone says, "Aha! There is a loving God who created me and I would be foolish not to repent and give Him my whole life!" Once that person does so, from that moment on, they are in a new kingdom quite different from the worldly one they previously knew.

Forgiveness, however, doesn't need a response in order to be imparted. In other words, Jesus forgave humanity at the cross whether they ever realized it or not. Everything has been paid—all the punishment for sin and disobedience—even if no one receives the free gift.

> *And if anyone sins, we have an Advocate with the Father, Jesus Christ the righteous; and He Himself is the propitiation for our sins; and not for ours only, but also for those of the whole world. (1 John 2:1–2)*

Forgiveness of sin has been extended to the whole world, even though the whole world may never be born again. God knew there was no way for us to come into His Kingdom unless He first wiped the slate clean on His own initiative, and that's what opens the door for us to receive our new lives. Therefore, the next time you are praying for someone and you feel the urge to forgive them of their sins, don't panic! You aren't saving them without their consent. You are doing the same thing Jesus and Stephen did; you are releasing a miracle. The forgiveness is already there, it just needs to be brought down from Heaven—which, by the way, is the same way a healing works. But that's another story.

Stephen and Paul

Let's go back to Stephen's death again. As we already saw, he gave his killers forgiveness before he let his spirit go to the Lord, and there was a very important man in that crowd of oppressors.

> *When they had driven him out of the city, they began stoning him; and the witnesses laid aside their robes at the feet of a young man named Saul. (Acts 7:58)*

Saul was the Church's worst enemy for a while; but a few pages after this event, he encounters the Lord and becomes the Apostle Paul. But it isn't a fluke that Paul's (Saul's) first mention is at Stephen's martyrdom. The two events are connected because of what Stephen released at his death. Because when Stephen died, Paul had an encounter with God. He saw a holy and loving man being brutally murdered while he glowed like an angel and released forgiveness. That demonstration opened a door for Paul to receive the gospel, and even if he didn't know it then, he was the recipient of an unseen miracle.

To grasp the significance of Paul's conversion, think

about how he persecuted the young church. The Bible says that he dragged men and women off to prison for their faith in Jesus, and it never occurred to him that he was doing something wrong. Paul thought he was doing God a favor by stamping out this new sect of Judaism.

Paul wasn't anti-God. He believed the scriptures and followed the law flawlessly, but the voice he was hearing wasn't the voice of the Lord. He had a form of God in his head that was ninety-nine percent true versus one percent lies, and he was under the influence of something that was definitely anti-Christ.

When Stephen was seized, the glory started to come out and then the heavens opened up above him. As we talked about before, Stephen was in a no-Antichrist zone. The only thing in the air over Stephen was the glory of God and ministering angels. Any wicked spirit who was influencing Paul had to depart for that moment, leaving his heart open to the truth of the gospel, perhaps even for the first time.

It will be the same in the last days. Christians will be killed every day for their faith; but because of their connections to Heaven, their deaths won't be in vain. Martyrdom will be another opportunity to release the glory and forgiveness, which will open the door for one last generation of sinners to come into the kingdom.

9

LOOKING AHEAD AND UP

Not too long ago, we had an event in America that gave us a small taste of what is to come. It was an outbreak of a strain of flu that became the news event of the month, despite its relatively minor impact. In many ways, it was like any other flu. It sickened and even killed people, but it was not the outbreak the media made it out to be. Nevertheless, rumors emerged of banks and schools closing, and we even heard talk of limiting travel.

I remember thinking, during that fiasco, "What would happen if this were for real? Would my family be all right?" I know in the last days we will all experience hardships in one form or another, but I started to wonder what my life would be like if it really happened. I was particularly concerned about healthcare and grocery stores. What would we do if they stopped working?

While this was going on, I couldn't help thinking back to some other recent catastrophes that crippled a portion of America. Hurricane Katrina came instantly to mind. I was driving across the country not long after that event, and I saw how gas and food prices were affected by a "localized" emergency. All that is to say that it wouldn't take much to disrupt American life as we know it. It is all hanging on by a very thin thread, and the panic that followed that "flu outbreak" made me think about the questions I asked in the previous paragraph.

The Lord used that opportunity to give me some very encouraging words. He said, "If a part of your society disintegrates, don't worry; it was only holding you back from a life of faith." Then He said, "You will experience more joy during that time than you do now." What a promise! Society, as we know it, could go down the drain and we would live a more joyful life because of it. It wouldn't be a case of our trying to be joyful amidst all kinds of hardships, either. We would be totally dependent on God, which would bring us closer to His glory and allow us to experience His supernatural provision. Being that close to Him would make for a joyful life.

However, I can imagine that time being absolute hell for people detached from God's presence. People will panic, commit suicide, and kill one another—all because they only know this physical life. Humanity will loose its collective mind when the material world crumbles around them. On the other hand, since the invitation into God's glory is free and presently available, there is no reason to wait. Just think what would have happened to Stephen if he hadn't paid attention to the heavenly realm. He could have lashed out at his persecutors instead of forgiving them. Or, he could have been so concerned with this material life that he caved in and renounced his faith.

Perhaps the most unsettling idea is being a Christian in the days of distress and having no way to cope with the adversity. Without a connection to God through the Spirit, you are left with only your physical body, which means that suffering and hardship will break your faith.

As in the dream about the Antichrist mentioned earlier, there will be a time when the mainstream, status quo Christian experience dries up. Many believers will fall away from faith in Jesus, and I wouldn't be surprised if the inability to cope with hardship would become the catalyst for that departure from the faith. Here is a description of that time from 2 Thessalonians:

> *Now we request you, brethren, with regard to the coming of our Lord Jesus Christ and our gathering together to Him, that you not be quickly shaken from your composure or be disturbed either by a spirit or a message or a letter as if from us, to the effect that the day of the Lord has come. Let no one in any way deceive you, for it will not come unless the apostasy comes first. (2 Thess. 2:1-3)*

Believers who have never learned to walk in the Spirit, who have never interacted with the unseen realm, will be easy candidates for apostasy. When the hardships come, their attachment to the physical body and the material world will throw them into disbelief and confusion, which will make them easy targets for an Antichrist regime that promises peace and even pretends to be Christ-like.

I am sure some Christians will be thrust into a dynamic faith in those days, even if they haven't given it the time beforehand, but why risk it? Why not start preparing now by learning to live in the Spirit?

Glory in the Family

For the last couple of years, I have had the recurring thought that someday I will be forcibly separated from my family. I believe God has given us all fair warning that the world climate is going to become hostile to believers, and I expect that will play out in my lifetime.

I encourage people to take a long, hard look at the Jewish holocaust in order to see how much the devil hates what God has chosen. During that persecution, families were separated, children were abused, and a part of society was treated as non-humans. Obviously, that is a very polite and understated description. But it brings out a good point. In the coming days, the world will not respect our rights at all. They will not think twice about ripping children from their mothers and dragging fathers off to prison. But before you think of this as just more gloom and doom, listen to the rest of the story.

The more I realized that hardship and persecution will be a reality, the more I became motivated to dive into God's presence. Also, I realized that it is essential for my children to experience His presence as soon as possible. As a father, I want to be sure that my kids know how to walk in the Spirit long before they need it to get through times of great distress. If the day comes when they are being dragged away, I want to look them in the face and say, "You all know how to experience Heaven right now. No matter what happens to you, and even if we never see each other again, go into the Spirit and rest in God's glory."

Not only will that allow them to face brutality, it will also let them be a last days witness just like Stephen. Even our children can look their oppressors in the eye and say, "Father, forgive them, they don't know what they are doing." For that to be a reality, it means we have to practice receiving God's glory as a family. We have to take the time to usher our children into His presence through worship and corporate prayer. The earlier they learn to allow the Spirit to lead them, the better. Therefore, everything that you have read about receiving His goodness and being in the Spirit applies just as much at the dinner table as it does in your personal prayer time. Encouraging each other as a family, and even praying in the Spirit together, will be a rich blessing.

A Quick Word about Being Prepared

There are a lot of Christians who won't hear any talk of going through hard times or living through an ultimate distress. They believe God would never allow them to suffer for His name, or they might have a misunderstanding of Biblical prophecy that makes them think it's a non-issue.

One extremely common belief is that Jesus will snatch us all to Heaven before things get really bad, thereby rescuing us from the trials of the last days. On the other end of the spectrum is the thought that the Church is going to increase and increase until it finally establishes God's government on earth, which would also eliminate the need for an end-times tribulation.

I believe both thoughts are seriously flawed in light of the scriptures, but that isn't the point I'm making. The fact is, there are many believers who aren't convinced they will ever have to deal with extreme persecution or disaster. Consequently, they will have no motivation to be prepared.

Personally, I believe you have everything to gain from expecting a period of severe distress, and I think denying it is extremely risky. If you are walking through life believing these harsh last days realities will never affect you, then you will be easily deceived and confused. On the other hand, having some prophecy-based expectation of the end will give you urgency, and that will always be a blessing no matter what happens to you. That's why it doesn't bother me to think about being separated from my family. I know God's forewarnings are to bless me, not stress me out.

After all, the last days aren't about God wanting us to suffer; it's about us realizing our fullest potential in Christ. It is a time for us, our children, and their children if God tarries, to be a glorious reflection of Jesus so that everyone who encounters us will encounter His love.

Looking Intently

Let's talk about Stephen again, one more time. We have already seen with Moses that when someone is glowing, it's because they are soaked with God's glory. And that will transform anything if given time. We know He can change our hearts because that happens to us everyday, but the same power will also change our physical bodies if we allow it.

In the first chapter about Enoch, we looked at how a lifetime of walking in God's glory prepared him to enter Heaven for good. His body was flooded with God's presence and he didn't have to leave it behind when he left. Remember also that it all happened because of what Enoch believed. He didn't have to do anything, he just had to fully believe and trust God. Like Enoch, Stephen loved and trusted God to an extreme, and the radiance coming off him tells us his body was already being transformed. I'm surprised the story doesn't end with Stephen disappearing into Heaven without a trace, because it seems like he was really close to an Enoch translation.

Going back to the passage about his death, something in there might give us a clue as to how Stephen prepared for that day. This is what happened right before they stoned him:

> *But being full of the Holy Spirit, he gazed intently into heaven and saw the glory of God, and Jesus standing at the right hand of God. (Acts 7:55)*

Here are some other ways to say "gaze intently."

- Eagerly look
- Strain or look with extreme concentration
- Fix the eyes with purpose

Stephen looked up into Heaven expecting to see something, and he did it on purpose. That should tell us it probably wasn't the first time he had seen into Heaven, since he already knew where and how to look.

You can practice looking into Heaven as well, so long as it doesn't become a chore or a religious ritual. We have already discussed a few different exercises that will help us get to know God's goodness, and the same ideas work with being in the Spirit. It might take some time to get comfortable with it, but God will do all the work once He sees you start to pursue Him.

The truth is, you don't live in apathy for a lifetime and then at your death suddenly start walking in the Spirit. You can only do it in the "clutch" moment because you have spent your life becoming familiar with the unseen realm. Stephen looked into Heaven in that instant because he already knew what an awesome place it was; and he knew it was where he could have unhindered communion with the Lord. If I'm going out like Stephen, I want to be able to look there, too.

All of us can learn to see into Heaven through the Spirit, and I use the term "learn" loosely here. The only thing that's needed is a surrendered heart and a desire for more of Jesus.

Start Looking Now

If you are longing to experience God in the Spirit but don't know how to get started, remember that all we have to do is simply *believe* Him. It also helps to know He can lead a lot better than we can follow. The Bible says that Jesus' love surpasses knowledge; and if you're like me, you feel compelled to try to understand it. However, the Lord put my mind at ease one day when He said, "It's not your job to understand My unfathomable love; it's My job to love you in a way that goes beyond all your understanding." The Lord is always trying to get us to trust Him more, and to rely on our own understanding less.

One more thing worth noting before we move on. Being in the Spirit is different for everyone because God is immensely creative. So, no two people will experience Heaven exactly alike. The Lord knows each of us so well, and will show us things that He knows will bless us. For instance, I love waterfalls. One of the first times I started to look into Heaven, He took me to see one in the garden. It was beautiful, and I found it to be the perfect place to talk with Him. But what is special to me may not be the same for you. You can expect Him to personalize your journey in a way that will make you realize you are the apple of His eye.

Don't worry about how it will happen or what might take place. Just give Him the freedom to reveal Himself to you, and remember that Jesus said it was to our advantage to know God through the Spirit. Also, give yourself the grace to experience God's glory on His terms, and don't try to come up with a list of steps to get into His presence. It is all about believing in Him and not about what you can do.

Even if you think it is not possible for you, give God the chance to prove you wrong. All you need to do is to ask Him to reveal Himself, and that will start the whole process going. Even if you have never interacted with the Holy Spirit before, you are just as capable of knowing His glory as anyone else.

If you need some help knowing what to do next, here is a quick recap of everything so far. It wouldn't hurt to go through these in order, and if you get to one that you haven't experienced or feel consistent in, work on that one for a while until it becomes an everyday standard.

᛫ If you have never done it, get immersed in the Holy Spirit. Let someone pray with you as soon as possible (preferably before you do anything else).

᛫ Give the Lord your own truthful assessment of your life. If you're apathetic, be honest about it. If you have trouble sustaining any passion for Jesus, just tell God like it is. Then, understand that God has a solution to complacency that has everything to do with His generosity and nothing to do with your effort. Being honest with Him goes a long way.

᛫ When you pray, give Him the space to love you. Take ten or fifteen minutes every prayer time and get comfortable receiving His doting words and affirmations. Having a quiet place helps.

᛫ Begin to envision your invitation into His presence. Let the Holy Spirit lead your imagination while you focus on His acceptance and love.

᛫ Trust the Holy Spirit. If you start to see something or hear something in the Spirit, give it a chance even if you aren't sure. The Lord will lead you better than you can follow. When in doubt, just focus on Jesus. He will take you on a journey if you let Him.

🐾 Don't get frustrated if your own thoughts and worries keep disrupting your time in His Spirit. There is no shame in Jesus, so give yourself a break. Take a deep breath, let God love you, and then see where He takes you.

Glowing with the Glory

At the end of the Lord's Supper in the gospel of John, Jesus offers a prayer for all believers. Take a look at what He says about His glory.

> *"Father, I desire that they also, whom You have given Me, be with Me where I am, so that they may see My glory which You have given Me. (John 17:24)*

Jesus never uttered a prayer that was outside of God's will, which is why everything He said was accomplished. Therefore, when Jesus asks for His followers to be with Him and see His glory, we can be sure that is exactly what will happen.

We know that will take place when Jesus returns, but we also have to consider that it's God's desire *right now*. He doesn't want to wait until we all get to Heaven for us to experience it, and he doesn't want to wait until the second coming to reveal His splendor. Whether it is Stephen seeing the heavens opened, or the Apostle Paul being taken up into the third heavens (1 Corinthians 12: 1-5), or the Apostle John being in the Spirit in the book of Revelation, we have seen historically that Jesus is not waiting to reveal His glory. It is the desire of His heart and He is eager to see it realized.

In the last days, a generation of Christians will let Him fulfill His desire in every way. They will receive everything He has for them, and it will transform them. They will all inherit eternity without the death of their physical bodies, so we can expect them to be radiant like Moses and Stephen even before they see Jesus coming in the clouds of Heaven.

Until then, we need to remember that Stephen was a person just like us; but he was so full of God's glory, that it started seeping out of his skin. Could the same thing happen to us if we gave God the chance to saturate us? Enoch was also a man just like us, yet he showed us what happens when a common person walks with God in intimacy.

I don't think there is any limit on what can happen when ordinary people are immersed in God's presence. There will be miracles, fearlessness, supernatural forgiveness, and we might even start to glow.

10

TRUSTING JESUS

If you need a little more encouragement to start walking down the same path that Enoch did, allow me to share one more testimony of being in the Spirit, beginning with a little background for this story.

I had been bogged down by recurring feelings of inadequacy and insecurity, and I kept thinking, "I'm not good enough, and there is no way I will ever be able to do what God has called me to do."

All of that surfaced one day while I was praying and I started to see a vision of myself inside of a prison cell, holding on to the cell bars. I could see Jesus standing on the other side of the bars, and He was holding a white key. Once I was ready to give up those bad feelings—and the lies that backed them up—Jesus gave me that key and I got out of the prison.

It took a while to finally release everything to Him; but once it happened, I found myself in the Spirit and dressed totally differently. I was wearing a long, white robe, and over that was a light blue garment with fine gold embroidery. I started to walk with Jesus down a translucent gold pathway. Over my head I could see the heavens, and underneath me I could see the lake of fire. As we walked, we started to float up into the heavens until we were suspended among the stars and planets. At one point, I saw Jesus open up His hand and in it were jewels and precious stones of all different colors. He scattered them out into the void and created more stars and worlds.

Then, He brought me to a communion table that seemed to also be floating in the heavens. To one side of the table was a gold set of scales with all of humanity in one bowl and a pool of His tears in the other. I sat down at the communion table and saw a stack of paper in front of me, and a pen in an inkwell. I felt in my heart that He wanted to write a plea to humanity, but I couldn't understand what He wanted to say until He came and sat by me at the table.

Then, I watched a sentence being written in cursive as if by an invisible hand. It said:

The only way to believe is to put all of your trust in Me.

As I sat there at the table next to Jesus, I could feel Him drawing me close; and when I looked into His face, I felt consumed by His unconditional love. The longer I looked, the more intense it got until I felt overwhelmed by His love and acceptance.

I think God's desire for all His children is for them to be completely restored by His love—and that really is all we need in order to be transformed. Most of our hang-ups in the faith develop because there is some area in which we haven't believed Jesus to be who He says He is. And therefore we haven't let His unconditional love saturate us.

Looking at Jesus and receiving a revelation of who

He is will take us from glory to glory. Nothing else is needed. So if you get frustrated in your efforts to experience life in His presence, just remember it isn't about your strength. It's about His.

Therefore, if you want to start walking down Enoch's path, all you need to do is believe. That's all Enoch did.

And the only way to believe is to put all your trust in Jesus.

Finis